Praise for
The Fortune Cookie Principle

"This should be the next book you read. Urgent, leveraged and useful, it will change your business like nothing else.
—SETH GODIN, AUTHOR, *THE ICARUS DECEPTION*

"The wisdom in this book is better than any fortune. Read and apply!"
—CHRIS GUILLEBEAU, AUTHOR, *THE $100 STARTUP*

"This book is an inspiration. Bernadette ignites real-world experience with a true passion for helping businesses move to the next level."
—MARK SCHAEFER, AUTHOR, *RETURN ON INFLUENCE*

"Full of inspiring stories about what makes businesses unique (and successful) in todays supersaturated markets."
—DAVID AIREY, AUTHOR, *WORK FOR MONEY, DESIGN FOR LOVE*

"It's so easy to overcomplicate what great brands and new businesses need to do to resonate with their consumers. The simple questions asked in this book help you to de-mystify that process. Had this book been available when I was driving Sales and Marketing Capabilities in my past corporate life at Cadbury Schweppes, it would have been recommended reading.
—WENDY WILSON BETT, CO-FOUNDER PETER'S YARD

"If you're someone who cares about why you do what you do and how you do it, this book is for you."
—TINA ROTH EISENBERG, FOUNDER OF TATTLY

The Fortune Cookie Principle

the fortune cookie principle

The 20 keys to a great brand story
and why your business needs one.

BERNADETTE JIWA

The Story of Telling Press
Australia

Published in Australia by The Story of Telling Press.

www.thestoryoftelling.com

Library of Congress Cataloging-in-Publication Data

Jiwa, Bernadette
The fortune cookie principle : the 20 keys to a great brand story and
why your business needs one / by Bernadette Jiwa
p. cm.
1. Marketing. 2. Business Development. I. Title.
II. Title: The fortune cookie principle

ISBN 978-1489583949

Printed in the United States of America

Book and Jacket Design: Reese Spykerman
Jacket Image: Veer

10 9 8 7 6 5 4 3 2 1

First Edition

For Moyez, Adam, Kieran and Matthew,
who are the best part of my story.

Contents

The Fortune Cookie Principle

New Marketing: A recap

The change in the way businesses must now work is not exactly news anymore. Author Seth Godin has been discussing the changing business landscape, New Marketing, and the importance of stories since 2002 (see *Purple Cow*, *Free Prize Inside*, and *All Marketers Tell Stories*). Just in case you've been out of the loop, though, here's what you need to know:

Attention is harder to get and keep now. We live in the opt-in age, a time when people can scroll on by, ignore advertisements, change channels, and avoid your marketing if they want to. In theory, people are easier to reach, but in fact, they are harder to engage. And while there are new ways of connecting with everyone and anyone online—through email, blogs, Facebook, Twitter, and so on—these tools can bring their own distractions.

Advertising is not marketing. A double-page spread in the weekend newspaper is not marketing. A promoted tweet is not marketing. A billboard at the train station is not marketing.

Marketing is not something that's tacked on at the end. It's no longer good enough to say, "We've invented this new kind of software; now let's hire a really expensive creative team to tell a story about it."

Real marketing is built into what you do and why you do it. It's part of your story, something that you do organically when your business is aligned with your mission and values. Kept promises, free returns, obsession with the details, returned emails, clean tables, and attentive staff—all of this is your real marketing. Real marketing creates a deeper impact, leaves a lasting impression, and is as powerful as a smile.

Having the market's attention is not enough to guarantee success. According to Brian Solis, just seventy-one companies from the original *Fortune* 500 compiled in 1955 remain on the list today. And generations of families capturing "Kodak moments" on film couldn't save Kodak from its downward spiral. The company filed for Chapter 11 bankruptcy in 2012. That same year, the four-person team who built the photo-sharing app Instagram, and gave their product away to millions of people for free, was acquired by Facebook for a record-breaking billion dollars.

Everything we knew about brand equity, it seemed, had finally turned on its head.

Introduction

In 1997, a young CEO was launching a new product, and here's what he said to his team:

"Marketing is about values. … Our customers want to know … what it is that we stand for…. And what we're about isn't making boxes for people to get their jobs done, although we do that well. … [We're] about something more than that. … we believe that people with passion can change the world for the better."

Then he played the "Think Different" advertising campaign video, which began with the words, "Here's to the crazy ones…."

The ad, of course, was for the Apple computer, and the "crazy ones" were people who dared to think that they could change the world. Steve Jobs went on to lead the company as it developed the iMac, the iPod, the iPhone, and the iPad and, along the way, made Apple the most valuable company in history. Apple changed how we buy and listen to music and the way we work and shop. How we consume media and the way we live and communicate. Apple even changed how we wait for the train in the morning, white ear buds in, fingers poised over screens.

Steve Jobs didn't give us a 32MB music player. He gave us 1,000 songs in our pocket. He didn't give us video calls. He gave us FaceTime with Grandpa. Apple forever changed how we feel about technology by becoming part of *our* story. That, in turn, changed how we think and what we do. Not many people accept boredom as an option these days. They are connecting to friends on Twitter while shop assistants check out their groceries. I saw a girl at the gym yesterday check Facebook between tracks in a Body Pump® class.

The way in which Apple communicates its brand story at every level—with a big purpose, good leadership, great design, and a user experience that people love—is what makes their products magical. The whole story, including that of the Mac user who sees himself as a non-conformist creative, or the teenager who wants to be connected to her "social graph" 24/7, combined with cutting-edge technology and Apple's design genius, is what makes people not just buy, but "buy into," the Apple brand. Yes, Apple changed our relationship with technology. But more importantly, the company changed how we feel about ourselves in the presence of their products.

This isn't another business book about Apple, though. It's about shining a light on some of the things that companies like Apple do to tell a great brand story. And it's about setting you on the path to telling your brand story and doing it well.

HOW WILL YOU MAKE ME CARE?

Even a four-year-old entrepreneur with her first lemonade stand knows that it doesn't matter how good your idea is if nobody knows about it. It's not enough just to set out your stall. And yet in business that's exactly what we do. We take our idea, our product, our innovation and expect people to pay attention to it. We try to change what people think (using the facts), so that we can change what they do (buy our products and services). Today, people have more choices than they need and they can simply ignore the things they don't care about. Changing how people think and getting them to act isn't so easy anymore.

How did Apple succeed where so many other technology companies have failed? I think what Steve Jobs hit on back in 1997 was the secret to spreading ideas. I call it "The Fortune Cookie

Principle." Every idea, every innovation, every product and service has two elements: the cookie and the fortune.

The cookie is the commodity, the utility, the tangible product. The cookie is the thing you put in the shop window and it has a fixed value.

Then there's the fortune, the magical, intangible part of the product or service, which is where the real value lies in the hearts and minds of the customer. The fortune is the story, the thing that makes people feel something. The real reason they buy the product in the first place. It's your purpose, your vision and values manifested. It's also the customers' story and world-view reflected back to them. The fortune gives the product an acquired value or a different perceived value.

People don't buy fortune cookies because they taste better than every other cookie on the shelf. They buy them for the delight they deliver at the end of a meal. Marketers spend most of their time selling the cookie, when what they should be doing is finding a way to create a better fortune. Of course your job is to bake a good cookie, the very best that you can, but you must also spend time figuring out how to tell a great story.

BUILDING A BRAND VS. SELLING A COMMODITY

> *"[G]reat brands are the ones that tell the best stories. Sure, good products and service matter, but stories are what connect people with companies."*
> —JASON FRIED, CO-FOUNDER, 37SIGNALS

Ideas spread, products become irreplaceable, and businesses grow when they stop being mere commodities and have meaning attached to them. It's not possible to be a brand and a commodity all at once. Customers don't demonstrate loyalty to commodities, but they can fall in love with a brand.

PRODUCT - MEANING = COMMODITY

PRODUCT + MEANING = BRAND

Stories are how we attach meaning and significance to anything, including businesses. When the five (or more!) bricks-and-mortar shoe stores at your local shopping mall were telling a story about waiting in line to see if your size was in stock so you could try on the shoes you'd selected, Zappos, the online shoe store, told a story about delivering "wow through service," with free shipping both ways and 365-day returns.

When Borders had floor upon floor of books you could touch and one that you might want to buy, Amazon created meaning for customers by offering a level of convenience and personalization that no physical bookstore could match. It was difficult to compete with a store that discounted prices and never closed. One that had every book in stock and available to be delivered directly to your door in just 24 hours. And a store that made recommendations to you based on your taste and shopping habits.

When Gillette had the endorsement of famous athletes like Roger Federer and David Beckham, Dollar Shave Club had a story about the truth.

In March 2012, Dollar Shave Club, founded by Mark Levine and Mike Dubin, launched a subscription-based, mail-order razor service with just $45,000. They had a good product built around a great story—"stop paying for shave tech you don't need." The startup launched with a promo video titled "Our Blades Are F***ing Great" that cost only $4,500 to make and went viral, with over 10 million views on YouTube to date. It was enough to make a Gillette marketing manager weep. Within a week, Dollar Shave Club had over 17,000 subscribers. Not just one-time customers, but subscribers who had signed up to give the Club repeat business for months and years to come.

Think about that for a minute. Razors and blades are perhaps the ultimate commodity; blades get dull and are tossed after several uses, and you can even buy entire razors that are disposable. Dollar Shave Club's business took off because they told a true story that matched the worldview of potential customers—apparently a lot of men resent paying for expensive razors in order to get the kind of shave they want. This startup made their customers feel smart for switching, by reminding them that a big chunk of the price they paid for razors from established brands was used for marketing and celebrity endorsements and was not necessarily linked to a superior product.

Dollar Shave Club also added convenience to the mix by selling their razors by subscription. Customers wouldn't have to remember to pick up a pack of razors at the supermarket and would never run out of sharp blades.

To put the Dollar Shave Club success story into some perspective: in 2010, $185 million was devoted to marketing the Gillette brand.

THE STORY IS YOUR ADVANTAGE

> *"Whoever tells the best story wins."*
> —ANNETTE SIMMONS

This is the whole truth, and it scares all kinds of people, from creators to scientists, from fledgling entrepreneurs to established brands. The product with the most features and benefits doesn't always win. It's not enough to be bigger or better, and that frightens us because our understanding of the world comes from what we were taught at school.

The best students get the best scores, get places at the best universities, get the best jobs, have the best lives.

That's a myth. Every day, people who are "good enough" succeed because they tell a better story.

It seems easier to sell features and benefits.

The facts.

Things we can easily explain.

A concrete advantage.

But tomorrow, anyone can build and sell a better widget for cheaper than you can do it today. There's another genius across town writing code as elegant as yours. Your job, then, is not just to build a great thing but also to care enough to tell the best story you can tell about it.

People don't buy your widget, your app, your code, your smart phone, your music player, your homemade cupcakes, your fresh flowers, your candles, your music, your computers, your front-row seats, your business-class flights, your graphic design, your printing, or your coaching.

They buy how it makes them feel.

The story is your advantage.

SAY HELLO TO THE KICKSTARTER GENERATION

The Internet, the PC, and mobile devices allow us to reach out to people in ways that we could never have dreamt were possible just ten years ago. Today if you want to invent and fund a new kind of pen, you don't have to be a hundred-year-old company like Parker, with a worldwide distribution channel. Now you can bring the story of your product directly to the people who might care about it, and you can make them care by telling a better story.

Ian Schon, a young engineer from Boston who developed a passion for product design, began wondering why he never carried a pen with him everywhere, as he would his car keys or phone. Ian set about designing a pen that was the sort of writing implement you'd carry with you every day.

Ian created The Pen Project and launched it on the crowd-funding platform Kickstarter, blitzing his $1,000 goal and raising $68,261 with a four-minute video. He told the story of his idea and described how he was making it happen. He talked about why he wanted to create this particular pen. (He wanted a pen that was "dependable, compact, durable, leak-proof, [and] easy to hold and write with.") He showed his passion, and he explained the prototyping process and the materials he was using. Ian mentioned how important it felt to shake the hands of the people who were responsible for manufacturing his pen locally and helping him bring his idea to life. He shared his belief that "the wearing of objects should be something that makes them valued," rather than needing to be replaced, and he urged us to care, too, with an insanely compelling value proposition about a pen "that people would buy once and use forever." A pen that he hoped would "outlast the user and be passed on."

WHAT IS A BRAND STORY?

A brand story is more than a narrative. The story goes beyond the copy on a website, the text in a brochure, or the presentation used to pitch to investors. Your story isn't just what you tell people. It's what they believe about you based on the signals your brand sends. The story is a complete picture made up of facts, feelings, and interpretations, which means that part of your story isn't even told by you.

Everything you do, from the colours and texture of your packaging to the staff you hire, is part of your brand story, and every element of it should reflect the truth about your brand back to your audience.

If you want to build a successful, sustainable business, a brand that will garner loyalty and, if you're lucky, become loved, you have to start with your story.

WHY YOU NEED A STORY TO TELL

"Stories also create value. If you take a simple object and build a story around it, the value increases exponentially. People shop with their heads and their hearts, and they will pay for an object based on how much it means to them."
—RICHELLE PARHAM, CMO, EBAY

As I mentioned earlier, without a story you are just another commodity. A replaceable cog in the consumption machine. But creating a brand story is not simply about the need to stand out and get noticed. It's also about building something people care about. Brand storytelling is about standing for something and striving for excellence in everything your business does. It's about framing your scarcity and dictating your value. It's about thinking beyond the functionality of products and services and creating a sense of loyalty and meaningful bonds with your customers.

A brand story is not the same as a catchy tagline that's pasted on a billboard to attract attention for a week or two. It is the foundation of your brand and a strategy for future growth. And it's the compass that gives a company the confidence to communicate what it stands for and why.

And once the story is baked into your brand, you don't have to worry so much about tactics. If you build a magnetic brand from the outset, you don't need to keep figuring out how to reinvent a strategy to raise awareness.

Story is how Starbucks created a whole new coffee category and elevated itself above its competitors. That story is the reason my client Kelly drives four kilometres every morning, passing Dunkin' Donuts and 7Eleven on the way to pay three times more for a cup of coffee. Starbucks didn't set out simply to sell coffee at premium prices; their mission was to be "the third place" (a social setting separate from home and the workplace). Every element of the Starbucks story, from the design of the chairs to the language used to describe their products, supports that mission. (*Venti* was once just a number in Italian; now it's a 20-ounce coffee and part of the Starbucks myth.) Brands like Starbucks and Apple don't deal in commodities.

Today your audience chooses the messages they want to hear. *They* decide what to share and how they share it. And they now have the platform and the digital megaphone with which to spread ideas they care about.

So give people a good reason to use that megaphone—give them a great story. A story that can change how people feel, one that connects your customers emotionally to your purpose first, and to your products and services later. A story that makes everything you do better. You have the opportunity to tell the story of your business to the people you want to hear it. You get to shape the kind of brand you'd like to become. You can build your business for the customers you really want to serve.

TOP-OF-MIND VS. CLOSE-TO-HEART

Branding is...

> *"The process involved in creating a unique name and image for a product in the consumers' mind, mainly through advertising campaigns with a consistent theme."*
> —BusinessDictionary.com

Branding in the traditional sense was designed to create recognition and awareness of commodities. It was the way businesses persuaded customers to decide. There's a difference, though, between branding and becoming a brand. A distinction between recognition and significance. It's possible to sell a lot of breakfast cereal through brand recognition. But if your brand isn't loved, then it's replaceable.

As Malär, Krohmer, Hoyer, and Nyffenegger point out, "The feelings that a brand generates have the potential to strongly differentiate one brand from another, especially as consumers usually emotionally attach to only a limited number of brands."

Branding might enable you to be top-of-mind. But top-of-mind isn't the same as close-to-heart.

Ask Microsoft.

HOW THE TWENTY KEYS CAME TO BE

I was a child of the TV-industrial complex. We had no telephone, but we did have a TV with three channels and no remote control. Our lives were slotted in around the scheduling of the TV channels. Saturdays began when the cartoons came on. The adverts were seen as information, not interruption. They taught us what to want. We knew that if you wanted a break, you should "have a KitKat," that the "lady loved Cadbury's Milk Tray," and that we should buy Diet Coca-Cola "just for the taste of it."

In the '70s, when my little brother was eight years old, he developed an obsession with Action Man toys. He'd get a new Action Man or outfits and accessories every Christmas and birthday. He began collecting the stars on the back of the packaging, which could be redeemed for more accessories. I remember going with him one day to help him choose how to spend his birthday money. As we went through the Action Man display, we discovered that the collectible stars had been ripped off every single box and piece of packaging. Those cardboard stars had become more valuable to little boys than the Action Man and the toy grenades inside the boxes.

In those days, a brand used to be a logo and a market position. Whoever had the most money to tell their story won. During the past few years, while I watched brands like Borders and Kodak lose traction, I began to wonder what made businesses relevant anymore. What determined the success of a brand in the digital age? Everywhere I looked, I was reminded that success was less about dominance and more about significance. Successful brands like Instagram, Starbucks, and Amazon were built around the effect they had on people and the impact they made in their lives. Significance, it seemed, was achieved by reaching out to customers differently on every level. Businesses that succeeded focused on more than their logo, inventory, and platform.

I began dissecting what it was that made customers love these brands and how they found ways to affect their customers. I combined those insights with my experience of working with companies and entrepreneurs to tell the stories of their brands.

And so the "Fortune Cookie Principle" was born. This is a brand-building framework and communication strategy consisting of twenty keys that enable you to begin telling your brand's story from the inside out. It's the foundation upon which you can differentiate your brand and make emotional connections with the kind of clients and customers you want to serve. It all begins with telling the truth and asking questions. It's not meant to be prescriptive. It's your starting point. There are some keys you will want to focus on more than others, depending on the type of business you are in.

While many of the examples in this book are household names and brands that you know and love, the twenty keys can be used as a framework for creating a brand story that informs strategies for any size of business. It's as applicable to a solopreneur selling her handmade cards on Etsy.com as it is to a *Fortune* 500 company that's trying to make sense of its message.

The most successful brands in the world don't behave like commodities, and neither should you. They build their brands around a big vision for the people they want their customers to become. A great brand story will make you stand out, increase brand awareness, create customer loyalty, and power profits.

Before you can tell your brand story, you need to develop it. Before your audience can share it, they need to understand and care about that story. You need a framework and a place to start. While Google has made it easier than ever to search for answers to almost anything, the truth about your story and how you will make your business succeed lies with the answers to the questions you perhaps haven't asked yet.

This is why I've included questions at the end of each of the twenty keys. They are designed to help you dig deeper, not to be an exhaustive list of checkboxes that you're done with when you get to the end. Feel free to add and ask more questions of your own. Nobody understands your business better than you do. You know its potential; you know what it could be in the world. It's your story. Go tell it.

Truth—What business are you in?

If every business is built around satisfying a customer's need, then every brand story begins at the intersection of your business's truth and the truth about what your customer needs or wants from you. The most successful brands show customers what their businesses stand for by communicating that truth in everything they do.

So what do I mean by "truth"? Well, the "truth" in this context is not just the collection of facts, figures, and nutritional values that are printed on your packaging (although that's part of it). The truth is a real understanding of the business you're in, which often has less to do with the product you are selling or the service you are providing and more to do with the feelings your brand elicits. Car companies don't build cars to be just functional and safe; the companies work hard to help customers to feel a certain way. Porsche understands that its customers want a very different experience than Volvo drivers do. Your customers may want to experience a feeling of excitement or safety. They might want to feel more healthy or happy. Perhaps they just want to feel like they are part of something bigger than themselves.

Understanding what business you are in and why that matters to customers is what enables you to differentiate your brand. That understanding helps you to narrow the focus of your business strategy. If your purpose is to delight customers with the best customer service on the planet, for example, then your strategy will revolve around hiring, training, and retaining the best staff.

Understanding the business you are in is the first step toward making your product or service something that the market values beyond its utility. Good businesses become great brands when their truth intersects with the truth of what it is their customers really want. And every business has to contend with the paradox of the customer's truth, which is brilliantly articulated by Rob Walker in his book *Buying In:* "We all want to feel like individuals. We all want to feel like a part of something bigger than ourselves." Telling a true story that supports that customer worldview has been the foundation of iconic brands and successful businesses since long before the Nike "swoosh" became a symbol of achievement.

> *"People don't want to buy a quarter-inch drill. They want a quarter-inch hole."*
> —THEODORE LEVITT, HARVARD BUSINESS
> SCHOOL PROFESSOR

KEEP YOUR CHIN UP

The hot tarmac of a filling station forecourt was a strange place to have an epiphany, and yet that's where the seed of the idea for Jimmy's Iced Coffee came to Jim Cregan on a hot Adelaide afternoon. Jim and his partner were road-tripping around Australia, and while he was paying for his fuel that day, Jim bought his first ever iced coffee. He guzzled the whole thing then and there on that hot tarmac and went back inside for another. So began a summer-long love affair with iced coffee.

Jim was so taken by the drink, which he found so refreshing after a surf and so energizing on a long road trip, that he contacted the company four times, asking if they would allow him to franchise their brand when he returned to the UK. After his

fourth flat-out "no," Jim decided to take matters in
hands. When he returned to the UK, he began res___
market, and he found that there was nothing like the quality of
iced coffee he had come to love in Australia. Jim persuaded his
sister Suzie to join him as a partner, and together they founded
Jimmy's Iced Coffee.

In November 2010 they set to work at Suzie's café, which became their late-night laboratory. They wanted the Jimmy's brand
to represent their values and to stand out from their competitors
with better ingredients, packaging, and branding. The original
package design was a classic retro shape, and by using that along
with distinctive typography and the colours they chose, Jim and
Suzie created an uplifting brand aesthetic (not what you'd expect
to see in the milk section of your local supermarket). Jim made
sure that the brand's unique voice was carried over into the copy
on the packaging, too.

The plan was to deliver joy to people who "wanted more than
ingredients in a vessel," so everything about the brand had to
deliver on that purpose. Jim and Suzie wanted Jimmy's to have
as few ingredients as possible (less than the seventeen they had
seen some brands use). So the Jimmy's recipe was made using
British milk, ethically sourced coffee, and demerara sugar. In
just five short months, coupled with a huge amount of effort,
Jim and Suzie chose a name, formulated their recipe, and found
a manufacturer. In April 2011, in the middle of a terrible British
recession, Jimmy's Iced Coffee launched with a double bass playing in the background and people dancing in the food hall in
Selfridges department store.

The brand's cool retro branding and positive tagline, "Keep your
chin up," continue to make people smile, as does the way the
founders get the word out about their product. Jim has been
known to jump out of his car in a traffic jam to knock on car

windows and pass a Jimmy's Iced Coffee to the drivers, asking them to try it and let him know what they think on Facebook and Twitter. He meets potential customers where they are, whether they're surfers in car parks by the beach or students at festivals.

"We want to produce really good iced coffee, but it's not iced coffee that we sell. We sell happiness in a carton. Being able to package and sell optimism is a rare art and I think we've managed it."
—JIM CREGAN, FOUNDER OF JIMMY'S ICED COFFEE

Jim has found that people love to connect with the face behind the brand, both in real life and online, and he sets out not just to get the product into their hands but also to deliver "little moments of joy." Every tweet and Facebook update comes directly from Jim. He loves the fact that he can "talk directly to customers without having to go through a crappy magazine." I've watched YouTube videos of Jim heating up a Gingerbread Jimmy's with a hot poker and keeping his chin up while sitting with a friend enjoying an iced coffee in the middle of a downpour as cars drive through puddles and soak them.

Two years on, Jim and Suzie have launched their product into hundreds of stores. They have taken their brand from zero to a turnover of £250,000 and expect that figure to quadruple this year to a million pounds. At a time when people are doing it tough in the UK and watching what they spend, Jimmy's has managed to capture the hearts of people by delivering more than just a commodity.

BETTER ISN'T ALWAYS BEST

In his book *Grow: How Ideals Power Growth and Profit at the World's Greatest Companies*, Jim Stengel, ex–Chief Marketing

Officer of Procter & Gamble, explains how he and his team in Europe turned the flagship brand Pampers around after it began losing ground to its competitors.

In 1997, Pampers, the original disposable nappy, had global annual sales of $3.4 billion, but the brand wasn't gaining market share. The less established and cheaper Huggies brand became the bestselling nappy brand in the U.S. and threatened to do the same in the UK and Europe.

Jim was given the task of finding a solution at Pampers Europe. He and his team analyzed Pampers' heritage and its strengths and weaknesses. When Pampers was first conceived by P&G researcher and grandfather Vic Mills in 1956, the brand was about providing convenience, saving time, and helping mothers to bring up their babies. But as the disposable-nappy category grew and competitors came on board, Pampers began to focus on the facts. The concrete advantages of their product above its competitors were absorbency and dryness. The research and development team obsessed about the dryness advantage. Dryness was "first, last and always." And while P&G's research suggested that mothers believed in the functional benefit of Pampers, they were still buying more Huggies.

The team at Pampers continued to innovate with improved comfort and fit, but they failed to link these innovations, such as breathable side-liners, to the truth about how their customers wanted to feel. The leadership team at P&G began to recognize that Pampers' brand values and development were driven by the engineers whose job it was to improve absorbency and dryness, instead of being driven by the needs and wants of customers. When P&G first introduced Pampers, they were a mother's lifesaver, freeing her from the drudgery of washing nappies. Then Pampers transitioned into a brand that talked at her with product-demonstration-style advertising, instead of listening to and engaging with her.

P&G had been measuring customer satisfaction on dryness, and the results had blinded the company to the other things that mattered to the mums they wanted to reach. In the end, the company had to admit that they didn't truly understand what mums *really wanted*—what their customers' truth was. Jim Stengel and his team realized that the way the company was differentiating its product just wasn't working, because Pampers' market share and profit margins were eroding. "Dryness was a means to an end, not the end in itself."

P&G went back to the drawing board to learn the truth from their customers about how the company could help modern families. By using focus groups, going into their customers' communities to speak with them, and immersing themselves in the lives of modern mothers in their homes, workplaces, and supermarkets, they found that what mums cared about most of all was their babies' development and the stages of change that happen in the first three years of their babies' lives. So P&G provided information and reassurance in the form of growth charts and parenting tips, as well as great products.

The company began to see that they could partner with mums in the development of their babies at each stage in those first three years. That new brand truth informed the innovation responsible for better product ranges, like the Baby Stages nappies, a group of products tailored to a baby's age and stage of development. The product-design needs of a newly crawling baby are different from those of a toilet-training toddler, and the new product range reflected that. Pampers began having a different kind of conversation with mums in its marketing and started sharing research and information about things they cared about, like pregnancy, childbirth, and child development, that had a positive impact on how mothers raised their babies.

If you look at the Pampers website today, you'll see less mention of the products and plenty of helpful advice about common concerns new mothers have about child care and baby development. By determining the truth of what their brand could mean to customers, P&G delivered a better product, enhanced the customer experience, created loyalty, and increased revenue to $10 billion a year globally.

So why should you care about uncovering the truth of your brand story? Because you get to choose what business you're in. You can be in the disposable-nappy business and sell dryness and convenience, or you can be in the "helping and reassuring new mothers" business and provide information about those crucial first few years of a baby's life. You can choose to be a commodity, or you can ask the question "What are we really selling?"

QUESTIONS FOR YOU

What business are you in?
Are you selling coffee or lifestyle? Renting rooms online or giving people the opportunity to connect and experience a city in new ways? Or…?

What do your customers want from you?
Would they like a product or support? Gym membership or improved health and wellness?

How do your customers want to feel?
Connected, informed, reassured, special, excited, happy, fulfilled, and on and on. Have you asked them?

What can you do to get them there?
Do your team members make an effort to remember regular customers' names and orders? Starbucks has a whole website, called mystarbucksidea.com, dedicated to getting customer feedback and suggestions. Does your website have a blog with comments where customers can share their views? Are you using social media to really listen to your customers?

Purpose—The reason you exist

> *"Disneyland is a work of love. We didn't go into Disneyland just with the idea of making money."*
> —WALT DISNEY

Of course you are in business to make money, but making money should be secondary to your purpose, a happy side effect of doing great work for people you care about serving. If you've mistakenly picked up this book looking for a shortcut to the money, thinking that "a story" might be it, I'm sorry. I know for sure that Amazon will give you a refund.

I've always believed that you should never do anything just for the money. Your work is too important and your time too valuable to spend it doing something you don't care about, just to have a fatter stack of dollar bills to count in the end. My gut told me that if you did something you cared about, the money would come. It's been true for me and for many entrepreneurs I've had the privilege of working with, and many more who have shared their stories with the world.

> *"[I]t's true that nothing I did where the only reason for doing it was the money was ever worth it, except as bitter experience. Usually I didn't wind up getting the money, either."*
> —NEIL GAIMAN, ADDRESSING STUDENTS AT THE
> UNIVERSITY OF THE ARTS

Even hugely successful organizations like Google believe that having a strategy for growth that focuses on more than a single bottom line is a worthy goal. It's all very well to have lofty goals,

you might say, but where's the proof that having a purpose-driv-
en brand strategy works?

Enter Jim Stengel (the P&G executive we met earlier) and his
groundbreaking research with research agency Millward Brown,
which looked at the most successful companies in the world over
the last decade. Together they uncovered something that should
change the face of business (I hope it does):

> *The Stengel Study of Business Growth ultimately identified 50
> brands with extraordinary growth over the 2000s relative to their
> competition. These Top 50 brands across all categories have created
> more meaningful relationships with people. ...*

> *In pure financial terms, the Stengel 50 as a whole grew three times
> faster over the 2000s than their competitors.... Individually, some
> of the fastest-growing of the Stengel 50, such as* **Apple, Google,
> and Pampers,** *grew on annual compounded average as much as 10
> times faster than their competition from 2001 to 2011.*

The fifty top performing brands, in good economic times and in
bad, were the ones that were founded on what Jim Stengel calls
an ideal. In other words, they had a bigger purpose, a mission
that the company set out to fulfil. For example, Google exists to
satisfy the curiosity of anyone with access to the Internet; Method, the household cleaning brand, wants to inspire happy, healthy
homes; and Jimmy's Iced Coffee delivers moments of joy.

Each of these ideals provides a reason for existing, beyond the
bottom line. Could it be that the way to build a thriving business is to do more works of love?

THE FIRST BRICK

"A company needs a unique reason to exist to get its strategy right."
—Jørgen Vig Knudstorp, CEO, The Lego Group

Lego, the sixty-four-year-old building system, was named Toy of the Century by the British Association of Toy Retailers in 2000. Just three years later, the company faced a budget deficit of more than $200 million and laid off 1,000 employees. In 2004, the deficit was in excess of $300 million. At the end of 2004, a new CEO, Jørgen Vig Knudstorp, was appointed. In 2005, the company returned a profit of over $110 million.

Jørgen, who has been dubbed "the man who rescued Lego," says that for two years he kept asking the same question: "What is the reason we exist?"

He spent those first two years as CEO figuring out what went wrong and getting back to the essence of what made the company unique. Jørgen believes that they lost their way because they forgot their unique reason for being—to "inspire and develop the builders of tomorrow." As the Lego mission statement says, "Our ultimate purpose is to inspire and develop children to think creatively, reason systematically and release their potential to shape their own future—experiencing the endless human possibility."

Before Jørgen came on board, the company had departed too far from its decades of heritage (the Lego brick and unique building system) and had begun to lose focus on its core business. The company had diversified into too many areas, like the Legoland theme parks, computer games, and apparel, too quickly, and they had failed to streamline their supply chain as they innovat-ed. The problems in the supply chain led to poor customer service and irregular availability of products because the company was geared toward serving smaller retailers and not behemoth businesses, like Walmart. According to Jørgen, it's because they had forgotten their purpose. The company estimated that it was losing $337,000 of value a day.

> *"[T]here is no building system like the Lego building system in the world. ... We had forgotten that. It's so obvious. It's so in your face, yet nobody in the company was talking about that. They were talking about how we could do things that were not that..."*
> —JØRGEN VIG KNUDSTORP

Focusing on the reason you exist informs everything your company does and drives the design of your business model. For Lego, it enabled them to focus on the quality of the moulding. The reporting in factories. The shipping and handling of more than 25 billion Lego pieces a year. In the '90s, the company had mistakenly focused on brand building, but by 2004 they recognized the need to shift their attention to optimizing operations in order to guarantee the supply of building sets to retailers. Amongst other things, the company streamlined the number of colours and the types of bricks and accessories that were manufactured, streamlined the number of suppliers they used, and moved distribution centres closer to customers. These steps enabled the company to be consistent in their decision-making and their operations.

Lego went from looking for opportunities for growth in other market segments and diluting its brand, to putting the focus back on the brick and the building system that children of the digital age still loved.

Revenues rose from $2.8 billion in 2010 to $3.4 billion in 2011. Sales grew 11% in 2011.

And it all started to come good by asking the simple question, "why are we doing this?"

"OUR TOWN IS GOING TO MAKE JEANS AGAIN"

That's the compelling statement which appears on the Hiut Denim website. And so the story begins with a purpose and we are drawn in. We immediately get the sense of urgency, of something meaningful being done here, something that matters, so we dive deeper.

The Hiut Denim Company, a manufacturer of bespoke denim jeans, is based in the tiny town of Cardigan (population 4,000) in Wales. For three decades, nearly 10% of Cardigan's population made 35,000 pairs of jeans a week for the Dewhirst company—until the Dewhirst factory closed down in November 2002. (Dewhirst closed several factories and moved production from Wales to Morocco to take advantage of lower labour costs.) The unemployment rate in Cardigan doubled overnight, and the "Grand Master" jean makers, with years of skill behind them, were left with no way to apply it.

Local entrepreneurs David and Clare Hieatt founded The Hiut Denim Company "to bring manufacturing back home. To use all that skill on our doorstep. And to breathe new life into our town." Their town is the reason they are in business and they have vowed never to make Hiut jeans anywhere else.

> *"We will have to tell our story every bit as well as we make our jeans."*
> —THE HIUT DENIM WEBSITE

Hiut's purpose isn't to persuade the guy who buys $30 jeans from a chain store and who thinks that paying $350 to wait six weeks for a pair of jeans is madness. Hiut's mission is *not* to make the most jeans, either; it is to make "the best jeans [they] can" for people who care about buying a pair of jeans that might last for years. In fact, Hiut started out making just two fits of jeans for men (and none for women yet) because they wanted to make sure they "got great at making jeans" before offering a huge range of styles. While Hiut sells directly to their customers, their jeans are also available in a limited number of small independent stores led by people who "understand [their] story, and have the time to tell it."

The fortune in a pair of Hiut jeans isn't just that they last longer. The company attaches a unique History Tag to each pair of jeans, and the tag's code is used to "tell the story of each pair" in the form of images (starting with those of the jeans being made) and updates that can be saved by the wearer on a private page at HistoryTag.com. David and Clare loved the idea of finding a way to make sure that "the memories created in [the jeans] never get forgotten."

Whatever your idea, whatever you market, sell, or promote—whether it's a cause, art, products, or services—one of the ways to differentiate from your competitors is to communicate your purpose. Products can be similar, but your purpose is unique.

Your job isn't to get people to buy your stuff; your job is to matter to them. You need your customers to believe in what you do. To "buy into" what you're about. Your business can help customers to express themselves. Your brand can become part of their story. You can shape culture, communicate beauty, stimulate thought, and inspire action. You don't have to be in business just to sell a pile of stuff.

"We are defined not by what we do but by why we do it. ... We need to understand our purpose, and without that we're just going to set up a company to make money to sell it. In a way, businesses need soul, too, and the why is the soul."
—DAVID HIEATT, CO-FOUNDER, HIUT DENIM

QUESTIONS FOR YOU

Why are you in business?
While Hiut exists to bring a whole town back to life, your business might exist to enable people to share experiences, to inspire people, or to enable people to fulfil their potential.

What can you do that nobody else can do?
How is your business unique? No company can make a building system quite like Lego's. Hiut Denim has craftsmen and -women with decades of skill under their belts. How about you?

How are you making sure that your business stays true to your purpose?
Do your employees know and understand what that purpose is and how it should affect how they go about everything they do?

How does doing business with you make your customers feel?
Do you want them to feel proud to wear or consume your product, happy to contribute to something that's bigger than themselves, more inspired to do the things they've dreamed of, or something else?

Vision

> *"Your vision of where or who you want to be is your greatest asset."*
> —Paul Arden

If your purpose is your "why," your vision is your "possibility." Your vision is your destination. It's a projection of the impact you want your business to have in the world. Your vision is a statement of intention about how you, your business, or your brand will influence the future. In part, your vision is your "big hairy audacious goal," to use the term coined by Jim Collins and Jerry Porras in *Built to Last: Successful Habits of Visionary Companies*. It is your dream of what could be.

A clear vision informs the day-to-day running of your business and shapes your strategy for the future. It focuses on the impact you will make on the lives of your customers.

The vision of the non-profit Room to Read clearly maps out the difference the organization wants to make in the world. As their vision document, "Envisioning Our Future: A Roadmap for Learning," says:

> *"Room to Read believes that World Change Starts with Educated Children. We envision a world in which all children can pursue a quality education that enables them to reach their full potential and contribute to their community and the world."*

They do a great job of honing it even further:

"Our goal for the future is more ambitious than ever: to enable more than 10 million children in over a dozen developing world countries to maximize their educational experiences by 2015."

Sometimes a brand vision is clear at the outset. Sometimes it shifts as the business matures and you begin to understand why your business exists and what it *could* be in the world.

FROM A COUCH TO A CASTLE

"Imagine if one day millions of people were living with each other in different cultures all over the world. What kind of world would that be? I think it would be a better one."
—BRIAN CHESKY, CO-FOUNDER AND CEO, AIRBNB

On the day of their graduation from Rhode Island School of Design, Joe Gebbia turned to his friend Brian Chesky and said, "I know that one day at some point in the future we're going to start a business together." Late in 2007, with just $1,000 in his bank account but ready to begin a new entrepreneurial life, Brian packed up his Honda Civic and headed to San Francisco, where Joe was living. When Brian arrived, Joe explained that the rent had been increased and was now $1150. Ah...

That same weekend, San Francisco was hosting an international design conference. You couldn't get a hotel room for love nor money. Brian and Joe put their heads together and came up with an idea that would solve their cash flow problem and rent short-fall, while helping people who were attending the conference. They decided to blow up a couple of airbeds and rent out the extra space in their apartment.

Brian and Joe needed to list their airbeds somewhere on the Internet, but since these people would be sharing their living room, they didn't feel happy about finding just anyone on Craigslist. So they decided to make their own website. It took them twenty-four hours. When they were done, they emailed some of their favourite design bloggers and got exposure overnight on some of the top design blogs in the world. They also got bookings from three guests—Kat, Amol, and Michael—who not only shared their room (helping them to make their rent that month) and their stories, but also inspired them to make AirBed & Breakfast a reality.

And so Airbnb was born from this kernel of an idea. Brian and Joe were soon joined by Nathan Blecharczyk, who became the platform's technical architect and third member of the founding team.

The trio began to think bigger. What if Airbnb could provide a platform for more people to rent out their spare space? The initial vision was a website that would advertise accommodations for conferences all over the USA. But their users quickly showed them that this vision was limiting. What about people who weren't going to a conference, who just wanted to book a room in Paris? The bigger vision became to give users the ability to book a room anywhere in the world.

Airbnb officially launched in August 2008, around the time of the Democratic National Convention in Denver (hotel rooms: 30,000), where Barack Obama would give his acceptance speech to 100,000 (great timing). As the idea caught on and the company grew, the founders began to realize that what they had built could be so much more than just another place to book a room online.

> *"As it turned out, there were many people out there looking for places to stay where the hospitality was genuine and the M&Ms didn't cost $6."*
> —AIRBNB WEBSITE

Today Airbnb is the place where you can advertise and book anything from a couch to a castle (or even shared space in a tent to be first in the iPhone line). Fifty percent of Airbnb hosts actually share the space with their guests during the guests' stay, giving travellers a unique local perspective. You can also rent cars, co-working spaces, and event spaces. Airbnb stimulates the local economy and helps us all re-create what Chesky calls "the sharing economy." The company's big vision is to "connect people in real life all over the world (millions of people) through a community marketplace."

As of February 2013, over 10 million nights have been booked in 192 countries. Airbnb has over 300,000 listings worldwide in 33,000 cities. More than 600 million social connections have happened because of the founders' vision.

"I can't yet say that Airbnb is going to change the world, but ... I can tell you that we're changing the way people experience it."
—JOE GEBBIA, CO-FOUNDER, AIRBNB

IT ALL STARTED WITH A BIRTHDAY PARTY

For ten years, Scott Harrison had made his living as a nightclub promoter in New York City. At twenty-eight, he had a Rolex, a grand piano in his apartment, and a girlfriend who appeared on billboards and in magazines. But his life had no meaning. Faced with what he calls "spiritual bankruptcy," Scott decided to find a way to live a life that was "the exact opposite" of what he was living at that moment. He volunteered for two years with a group called Mercy Ships, who brought medical care to the world's poorest. Working as a photojournalist for the group in Africa, Scott was tasked with creating a visual account of everything the organization did. He witnessed firsthand the realities of some of the world's poorest people—"those living on less than $365 a year." The kind of money Scott "used to blow on a bottle of Grey Goose vodka at a fancy club. Before tip." As he explains in an interview with Kevin Rose:

> *"I was storytelling for ten years; I was just telling the wrong story. I was telling a story that your life will have meaning if you get into my club, spend $1000, get wasted, and get laid. ... Now it's 'come join me in changing the world....'"*
> —SCOTT HARRISON, FOUNDER, CHARITY: WATER

Scott's work in Africa helped him decide to serve the 800 million people globally with no access to clean drinking water. He had several audacious goals for tackling a whole raft of problems, like poverty, health, and education, but soon realized that access to clean drinking water was the one thing that could change everything.

So in 2006, with no money and a little goodwill, Scott founded the non-profit charity: water by doing what he knew best. He threw a party in New York for his thirty-first birthday and invited 700 friends. The $15,000 raised that night created three new wells in Uganda and fixed three broken ones.

The following month, Scott and a team of a hundred volunteers created a travelling outdoor exhibition. They filled Perspex tanks with dirty pond water to demonstrate the reality of the choice facing millions of people every day. They sold $20 bottles of water at these outdoor exhibitions and raised both money and awareness in the media.

A year later, on his thirty-second birthday, Scott raised $150,000 by giving up his birthday celebration and asking people to donate $32 instead. This inspired the charity: water team to launch the September Birthdays campaign, which raised $1 million in its first year, giving 50,000 people in Ethiopia clean water. Just six and a half years after its launch, charity: water has funded over 8,000 water projects, giving 3 million people in the world's poorest countries clean drinking water.

The organization's big vision is their true north and they are well on the way to realizing it. Charity: water's vision:

> *"charity: water believes that we can end the water crisis in our life-time by ensuring that every person on the planet has access to life's most basic need—clean drinking water.*
>
> *In the short term, our goal by 2015 is to transform the lives of at least 10 million people by providing them with access to safe water."*
> —MO SCARPELLI, MULTIMEDIA PRODUCER, CHARITY: WATER

QUESTIONS FOR YOU

What effect will your business have on the future?
You don't have to set your sights on changing the world for millions, like Scott did. Think about how your work will change a tiny part of it for even the first twenty people.

What happens because you exist?
Paint a picture of the results you want to deliver for the people you want to serve. More of this and less of that?

How can you support this vision in the day-to-day running of your business?
Think about how you will align decisions on everything from the content of your email newsletters to scaling your business with this vision.

How will the changes your business brings about change how your customers feel and then act?
When you know how you want them to feel, you'll stay on the right track.

Values

I finally fell out of love with my favourite little café. Eighteen months ago I was going there almost every day, not just for the coffee but because of how I felt there, amongst the noise, the life, and the friendly faces, with the smell of the ocean wafting through the open windows. It used to be such a great place. All of the food was made right there on the premises and the owners were in the thick of it—caring—and that showed.

Last week I decided I'm not going back. Their success has killed everything they once stood for. It's crushed the soul (the thing that made it brilliant in the first place) out of the business. The café had been busy to the point of bursting for a long time. The great coffee (every cup), the homemade food, the values of the owners, and the way those values affected the staff meant that people loved telling their friends about the place. Customers didn't mind waiting for a table or paying a dollar extra for a delicious fresh brownie and the story they could tell themselves as they sat reading the morning paper. Then everything changed.

The business expanded. They extended their premises. The owners started working "on" the business, not "in" the business. Their new systems and processes changed the whole feel of the place and wiped the smiles off the faces of the staff. It became obvious even to customers that the goal posts had shifted, that the first focus was maximizing profit and capitalizing on the café's growing numbers.

It seemed that their values shifted along with their metrics. The owners forgot what made them successful in the first place, things like remembering regulars and taking a few extra minutes to connect and to be generous. Or perhaps they never really knew.

This doesn't mean that it's not possible to scale a successful business. It's perfectly okay to have a change in strategy as long as you don't have a change in values.

Our behaviours are shaped by our beliefs. Our values drive our actions, and companies are no different. If you don't know or acknowledge the beliefs that underpin your business, how can you know how to act? Values reinforce the vision for the business, shape its culture, and guide its behaviours. They enable a business to build trust and loyalty with its customers. Values even influence operational decisions. And they are a measure of the brand's integrity because you can't say one thing and do another. (Well, you can… but people won't like it when they find out.)

Values help to clarify who you are and what you stand for. Your brand values are anchors and guideposts for staff, helping to explain why you work the way you do. They influence customers' buying decisions because customers buy from brands whose values align with theirs. Shared values enable brands to become part of the customer's story, giving customers a way to express themselves. Values are the common ground on which businesses and customers unite. And as Jim Stengel proved in his work with Millward Brown, values-based businesses have healthy bottom lines, too.

> *"Consumers don't just want to understand the story. Increasingly, they want to be part of it…."*
> —ROBERT FABRICANT

NO COMPROMISE

In many ways, Aimee Marks was like any other eighteen-year-old Melbourne teenager about to start university—apart, that is, from a quest she was on that had begun as a design assignment for school. Aimee had been asked to find an area of packaging design that hadn't been disrupted in twenty years and to work out a way to improve upon something already in the marketplace. Her assignment led her to the feminine hygiene aisles of supermarkets. She took on the task of redesigning and improving tampon packaging. As Aimee was writing the list of ingredients on the back of her design prototype, she began to ask herself some searching questions that had never crossed her mind before. What was this stuff that she and millions of women in the developed world were putting into contact with the most intimate parts of their bodies each month? It turns out that the 12,000 (on average) tampons that women use in their lifetime are made with plastics and synthetics like polypropylene and viscose rayon.

Aimee couldn't see why it wasn't possible to make a chemical-free tampon. It took her six months to find one chemical-free brand hidden away on the bottom shelf of a health food store. This scarcity was something that Aimee felt just wasn't acceptable; she believed that women should have a choice. With financial help from a family friend who admired her passion, after months of research and following years of development with microbiologists, suppliers, and manufacturers, Aimee brought TOM Organic to market in 2010. She was twenty-three years old. TOM Organic tampons are made from "organic cotton—free from perfumes, chemicals, pesticides, bleach and genetically modified cotton." TOM Organic products "are made using the most sustainable, organic, biodegradable materials available." The business is created around what Aimee calls "a full-circle-of-values perspective," which is measured not only in the bottom line but also in how the brand impacts the lives of customers and the environment.

> *"Success is not just a commercial or economic figure. Success to us is how many women we have touched with our product. We have goals to touch over a million women in the next three years. We are encouraging our staff to celebrate wins around non-financial factors which ultimately lead to financial success. But that's not what drives us. It's a by-product of why we do what we do."*
> —Aimee Marks

Aimee has built the business by not compromising on her values, honesty, integrity, transparency, family, or culture. One of her goals was to take organic tampons off the bottom shelves of tiny independent stores and make them available to Australian women in the big two supermarket chains. She wanted to build a business that had a social impact, which meant that women didn't have to compromise on health and good design because of limited choices.

Three years on, the TOM Organic brand sits alongside mainstream feminine hygiene products, produced by global behemoths, in the big two grocery chains in Australia. The company has gone from zero to a million-dollar turnover in those three years. The business doubled between 2011 and 2012.

WHAT THE WORLD WAS WAITING FOR

In the spring of 2011, Tina Roth Eisenberg had just returned from a birthday party with her daughter, who was excited to find a temporary tattoo in her party goodie bag. Of course she wanted to apply it straight away. Tina baulked a little. As a designer from Switzerland (now living in New York and running the incredibly successful blog swiss-miss.com), she was really put off by the aesthetic of the badly designed and badly produced temporary tattoo. (She did, however, let her daughter apply it.)

Tina told me that she has a personal rule that if she finds herself complaining about something, she either does something about it or stops complaining.

"As I was sitting there while the tattoo was drying, I thought 'I can totally do something about this.'"
—TINA ROTH EISENBERG

Tina approached some of her design colleagues and asked them if they'd be interested in designing for skin and if they'd collaborate if she built a cool store. They were thrilled to be involved. Tattly Designy Temporary Tattoos launched online in 2011. Within minutes of its launch and Tina's blogging about it, orders began coming in from all over the world.

Almost two years on, Tattly has eight employees and more than 350 tattoo designs. The company ships to more than ninety countries and is in more than 400 stores. Tina says the journey from "idea to now is mind blowing." She had never made a product before and she didn't really know what the demand for Tattly would be, but she believes that Tattly's success is proof that "we should never shy away from challenging the status quo."

"The values of the founder trickle down in the product. As a founder of a company, you need to know what your values are and that they go across the board on every single detail of your product."
—TINA ROTH EISENBERG

It's easy to sense Tina's values when she talks about how she built the business, and it's easy to see them reflected in Tattly products. Tina's love of great design, her resourcefulness, creativity, and sense of fun, combined with integrity, authenticity, and respect for the people she works with and serves—all of these values shine through.

You know you're onto something when your customers start posting and sharing pictures of themselves adorned with your product (or your product adorning them) on their social networks. Ivy, who was at her friends' Melissa and Mark's wedding, posted on Instagram a photo of an "adorn yourself" display board at the wedding reception. The newlyweds gave away messages of love and happiness in the form of Tattly tattoos for their guests. I've seen pouting teens, pairs of friends, a guitar, wooden buttons, and naked babies all sporting Tattly tattoos on Instagram. And time and again in the comments, people ask, "Where can I get them?"

The value that Tattly delivers goes beyond the pixels and ink used to create the tattoo. It's in the feeling the wearer gets when she looks at it on her forearm and pulls up her shirt sleeve to show it to her friend.

Tina continues to partner with leading designers to create the beautiful temporary tattoos that the world didn't know it was waiting for.

QUESTIONS FOR YOU

What do you believe?
Make a list. There are no right or wrong answers.

How are you demonstrating your beliefs to the world and to your customers?
Do your values come across in the service you deliver and the tone you use in your content?

How is the world made better for your being here?
Brian and Joe from Airbnb know they are helping people to connect and to experience the world in new and exciting ways. What's your brand's legacy?

How do your values and actions make your customers feel?
The automated messages from MailChimp make me smile. Are you making your customers feel a part of something, happy, or loved?

Products and services

Let's think back to the fortune cookie (our product) for a moment. The cookie is the commodity, the thing that is exchanged with the customer for cash. Remember, the customer is not actually buying the commodity; she's buying the benefit it delivers. She's buying the joy of breaking the cookie open and sharing it with her friends at the end of the meal. Most (I hesitate to say all) products and services can have meaning attached to them. I often wonder about this idea working for six-inch nails, but even then I think it's possible. After all, it's been done with schools, seminars, blogs, pens, notebooks, glue, razors, juice, tax refunds (watch for the story later in the book), and small squares of paper that have a strip of glue on the back.

So while you've got to get the cookie recipe right, it's really important to make the fortune—the story—good, too. You need to give people a reason not just to buy your products, but to buy into your brand. The product must tell part of the story.

NOTHING ELSE

Back in 2003, in the little suburb of Balmain in Sydney, Tim Pethick started a juice company without knowing he was starting one. What began with Tim's passion for creating freshly squeezed juices and smoothies for his family in the morning developed into an obsession as Tim began to wake earlier to try new fruit blends. Soon he was staying up all night to experiment.

Tim couldn't understand why there wasn't a product on the market that was like the juice he produced for his family. Something made with just fruit and nothing else—no sugar, additives, or preservatives. When he couldn't find the product he wanted, he decided to create it for people who wanted to be healthy but were time-poor and were willing to pay for the convenience of having a real fruit juice prepared for them.

> *"[W]hen we started off in 2003 in Tall Tim's Kitchen we couldn't find a company in Australia that made juice from nothing but fruit so we did it."*
> —NUDIE JUICES WEBSITE

Nudie Juices started with Tim and his team of two in a small office in Balmain, plus a single stockist. They used 256 pieces of fruit that first week and sold forty bottles. Ten years on, the team of seventy needs 3 million pieces of fruit per week to supply over 5,000 stockists.

Nudie couldn't compete with the bigger players in the juice market on price, distribution, or advertising, so they had to compete by making a better product.

> *"We knew we had to come up with a solid gold product that was totally different and solved a key consumer problem. And that was nothing but fruit in a bottle, so if you didn't have time to blend fruit at home, we'd make it for you."*
> —JAMES AJAKA, CEO, NUDIE FOODS

There was nothing like it on the market in Australia at the time. The other juices on the market were made from imported, concentrated ingredients. Nudie's product was the story. It was also part of the story the customer could tell himself. And an easy story to share with friends.

WHAT'S THE VALUE OF TRUST?

I've never met David—in fact, we've never even spoken on the phone—and yet I trust him with the keys to my business every day. David provides me with technical support for my website. He's the WordPress guru at ClickWP.com who keeps my online business on the road. He's there to answer questions, fix bugs, and make sure that my site is backed up. Much like a truck driver with no truck, without my website and my blog I have no business. Working with David provides me with peace of mind, and it's hard to put a value on that. David has no shortage of customers who are happy to pay a monthly fee for that peace of mind. What David's built his business on isn't just great service; it's trust.

BUYING INTO THE LEGEND

There's nothing like the possibility of a blank page. A clean sheet waiting for a new idea to be fleshed out. Every artist, from Andy Warhol to James Joyce, began with the possibility of a blank page. In 1997, the Moleskine brand was created to bring back a certain kind of handmade black notebook which was bound in Paris and used as a creative tool by the avant-garde artists of the nineteenth and twentieth centuries. The brand had an instant cultural heritage, being linked as it was to those legendary creatives like Picasso who were said to have used a similar black notebook. Initially just 5,000 notebooks were produced in Milan by a small Italian company called Modo & Modo SpA.

Moleskine notebooks now enjoy cult status amongst creatives and travellers of all kinds, from illustrators to writers, app developers to filmmakers, who want to save and express their ideas on paper. The notebooks are a symbol of belonging to a tribe that understands the power and potential of a single idea. The brand has built a thriving community of devoted users at myMoleskine who inspire each other with their Moleskine artworks and share their notebook hacks with other Moleskine devotees.

Having built a following and a loyal customer base, Moleskine appears to have gone on to follow Seth Godin's advice:

> *"You don't find customers for your products. You find products for your customers."*
> —SETH GODIN

The company has extended its product range to planners, themed notebooks, signature pens, bags, and book lights. They have even created an app to enable creatives to find ways to intersect the physical notebook experience with the digital one.

When Maria Sebregondi, Vice President of Brand Equity at Moleskine, was asked what underpinned the success of the Moleskine brand, she said:

> *"We have a strong focus on storytelling. A notebook—the flagship object in our collection—typically collects stories. Avant-garde artists of the past used it to gather notes and sketches while in the streets, in cafés or while travelling. Everything we produce, from bags and pens to apps, stems from this history. We create tools to support creativity, to organize our time and ideas, against the backdrop of increased mobility worldwide. ... This is what gives us a unique cultural positioning."*

QUESTIONS FOR YOU

Why does the world need your product or service?
Tell the story of how your idea came to be and why it matters.

Why you? Why now?
I don't mean "what are your credentials?" although that might be part of it. What's the story of why you want to make this happen?

How will you do this better than anyone else?
Think about everything you're going to do to break what exists and challenge the status quo.

How can your story make the product better?
Can you use the truth about why you want to bring this product to market to help tell the story?

Your people

"YOU are the magic."
—Paul Arden

Your leaders and staff are the face of your brand. Often they are the front line of your brand story. Their job is to show the world what your business stands for. Their posture, their attitude, and their influence trickle down through the organization and affect it. A good leader maps out the vision for the business. She paves the way for others to follow. Your people power your organization in a way that all the technology in the world never can. They see the possibilities and are charged with both shaping and adhering to a vision. They implement the strategy and make the human connections that are such a big part of the brand's story. This principle applies to the two-person staff of a tiny bakery as much as it does to the Chief Marketing Officer at Coca-Cola.

Leadership not only drives culture; it can also have a huge impact on your bottom line. We've already seen the difference that outstanding leadership can have on a company; CEO Jørgen Vig Knudstorp began turning The Lego Group around soon after his appointment, and his leadership continues to drive results. In 2011, for the eighth year running, Lego captured significant market share in a sluggish toy market—their sales rose by 17% to $3.495 billion—and in 2012, they saw a 25% rise in revenue over the previous year. While the global toy market has been shrinking, Lego's sales have tripled in the past five years under Jørgen's leadership.

Every single person in your organization, from the cleaner to the designer, from the waitress to the CEO, has a role to play in touching your customer. Whom you hire, what they stand for, and how they show up all tell a story.

EMPOWER YOUR PEOPLE

"Our employees are our brand."
—KIMPTON HOTELS

Bill Kimpton introduced the idea of boutique hotels in the U.S., opening the doors of his first hotel in 1981. He wanted to create a new kind of hotel experience for American travellers. Bill wanted to change how people felt as soon as they walked through the hotel doors. He had a vision of a more intimate hotel experience.

"A hotel should relieve travelers of their insecurity and loneliness. It should make them feel warm and cozy."
—BILL KIMPTON, CHAIRMAN AND FOUNDER, KIMPTON HOTEL AND RESTAURANT GROUP

There is a secret to creating intimacy in any business. It's not done with pillow menus and Egyptian cotton sheets (even if they are nice touches). That secret lies in the moments of human connection, when we really see and touch the other person.

Kelly called ahead from the airport to the Kimpton Hotel in Chicago. She had a bad back and wanted to know if there was a drugstore close to the hotel so she could buy some Epsom Salts; she thought they might help soak some of the pain away. When she arrived at the hotel, the receptionist who checked her in told her that they had upgraded her room to a suite so that she would have a nice big bathtub to soak in. The receptionist also gave Kelly directions to the nearest drugstore.

An hour later, someone from room service knocked on Kelly's door. Kelly was presented with a tray laid out with a bottle of water, chocolates, and a box of Epsom Salts.

The handwritten card read, "Hope you get some time to relax while you're here. Let us know if you need anything at all. Wasn't sure if you were a fan of chocolate but I hear it cures everything."

It was signed by Erica (the receptionist) and several other members of the hotel staff.

The guy delivering room service smiled at Kelly's overwhelm. "We love to listen to our customers," he said.

No surprise, then, that according to the Market Metrix Hospitality Index™, "Kimpton has the highest customer satisfaction scores (93%+) and emotional attachment scores (89%) of any hotel company operating in the United States."

These kinds of results don't happen by accident. They are enabled by baking an ideal into the organization's culture and by empowering the people who work in your business to live up to that ideal. Kimpton Hotels' focus on service and customer care begins with a unique culture of finding the right people and making them feel valued. The company makes employees proud to work there because of its commitment to social responsibility, demonstrated by giving back to local communities and charities and with its comprehensive EarthCare Program.

Kimpton has been recognized as one of *Fortune* magazine's 100 Best Companies to work for. The company's people are their secret weapon.

*"We're rock-steady in our belief that it's our incredible cast of indi-
viduals who make our hotels and restaurants so special in [the] lives
of millions of guests, and we celebrate them constantly."*
—THE KIMPTON WEBSITE

They're not just saying that, either. Kimpton has embedded a
culture of caring in its organization by taking care of the people
who work there, offering health benefits, opportunities for training at Kimpton University, personal development and mentor-
ship programs, and diversity training. Kimpton also encourages
every member of the staff, from room attendants to managers,
to have an entrepreneurial vision and to bring to their work
their passion for the difference they can make.

*"We don't have a lot of fussy procedures and manuals lying about
telling us how we have to do something. We're compelled by utter desire to be the best human beings we can possibly be. Turns out, that's
good for business."*
—THE KIMPTON WEBSITE

LOVE WHAT YOU DO

If you send out newsletters by email, you might already know
about MailChimp. It's an online tool for designing and sending
email newsletters, managing subscriber lists, and tracking the
results of mailings. Businesses of all shapes and sizes (3 million
to date) use MailChimp to send email newsletters to their clients. The company's point of difference is that they work hard
to make fun a regular part of the customer experience, with
a cheeky monkey mascot named Freddie and lots of human
touches in their copy. If the less serious version of their user interface doesn't float your boat, you can switch to the more sombre Party Pooper Mode.

I was shutting down an old MailChimp account recently, and here's the message I got:

"Your account is officially closed. We're heartbroken to see you go. Could you spare two minutes to tell us how we could improve?"

The message didn't tell me that the company valued my feedback; it was more personal, more human. That message changed how I felt in the moment. And because I have had nothing but great experiences with MailChimp, I gave them two minutes of my time. One of the survey questions asked me how dealing with MailChimp made me feel. Of course they had me right there. When I was done answering, here's what the final message said:

"Thanks a million for taking the time to share your feedback. It's like gold dipped in frosting for us."

I've never dealt with a human being at MailChimp, but they make me feel as if I am dealing with a person... every time.

That takes the skill and caring of great people, supported by a culture that allows them to make a difference. MailChimp has created this culture by hiring the right people, who care about delighting their customers even though they may never shake their hands or look into their eyes. They have built humanity into their business. When a staff member is giving unscripted customer support from the MailChimp open office environment, a quick "resolution time" is never the measure of success. The company has empowered its staff to have conversations with customers, not just to resolve tickets. They want their team to live by their tagline, "Love What You Do."

"The culture of giving people 'permission to be creative,' has been one of the keys to MailChimp's success."
—CHIKODI CHIMA, FAST COMPANY MAGAZINE

At MailChimp they do things they don't have to do, like send T-shirts and Freddie-the-monkey knitted-hat giveaways to customers. MailChimp added a "Love What You Do" colouring book to their resources library just for fun.

"MailChimp's creative gewgaw giveaways aren't part of a master marketing plan, but rather the byproduct of a bunch of passionate people focused on delighting customers."
—JOSEPH FLAHERTY, WIRED MAGAZINE

It's no wonder that the company is adding 6,000 new customers a day.

QUESTIONS FOR YOU

How does your team uphold the vision and values of your business?
Think about things you do differently and about how you build on your vision and values as a team.

How do you hire for values, not just skills?
At Kimpton Hotels, "people get hired for who they are, not just what they have done." How do you know you've got a good fit and what's non-negotiable?

What difference do your leaders and staff make in the lives of your customers?
Describe the types of interactions that could happen and the results of them.

How do the words and actions of your leaders and staff make people feel?
Describe the feelings you want your customers to experience. Can the team you have and each member of the staff you hire pull this off?

Value you deliver

People don't buy what you do; they buy how it makes them feel.

On Valentine's Day, a single rose will set you back $8. Two days later, it's just $5. While you clearly get better value for your dollar after Valentine's Day, the market dictates that the roses are more valuable on February 14th.

The value of your product or service isn't just in the price you charge; it's what the customer perceives it to be. What makes something more valuable is the story the customer was able to tell himself after he left the florist's that morning.

It might appear that people buy the results that you promise or the benefits that your products and services deliver. In his book *Brainfluence*, however, Roger Dooley reminds us that, according to Gerald Zaltman and other experts, "[n]inety-five percent of our thoughts, emotions, and learning occur without our conscious awareness…." As Dooley points out, customers "generally can't understand or accurately explain why they make choices in the marketplace…." People aren't buying the facts about or features of your products and services. They might use these to justify their decisions, but your customers are mostly making choices based on emotions. They are buying the difference you make. The value you deliver is in the intangibles, the things that money can't buy. Feelings of connection, happiness, safety, fun, security, belonging, and love.

In business, we often get stuck figuring out what people will pay for, rather than what's valuable. Value has little to do with price. It's about the customers' perception of what the benefit is worth to them. It's your job to deliver something that they care about beyond the price. This is probably something your competitor is not offering. It might not be something customers can hold in their hands, but it's what every customer is happy to pay for.

To deliver value, then, businesses need to generously focus on what customers want and how they want it delivered. Real value, the kind that builds loyalty and a sustainable brand, is never about what the business owner happens to have in the warehouse and urgently needs to sell at a knockdown price. Value, like love, is in the eye of beholder.

"In the factory we make cosmetics; in the drugstore we sell hope."
—CHARLES REVSON, CO-FOUNDER OF REVLON

WHAT'S MORE IMPORTANT THAN THE COFFEE?

When is a café not a café? When it's a place where people come to play games with their friends, as much as they do to grab a bite to eat.

Snakes & Lattes is a board games café in Toronto with over 2,500 games customers can borrow for the evening to play with their friends. If they want WiFi, they're out of luck, but if they want to socialize, they're all set. Guests pay a cover charge to sit and play games for as long as they like (sometimes until 2 am on Friday and Saturday).

As an article in *Toronto Life* explained in 2010, French couple Ben Castanie and Aurelia Peynet got their business idea from their "memories of toy libraries in Paris ... and from a visit to a hobby shop in Chicago." The games at Snakes & Lattes—collected from "vintage shops, yard sales and toy stores"—are primarily family-friendly European-style games that don't eliminate players.

I've read five-star reviews from groups of people who waited for two hours in a pub down the street or in the sandwich shop across the road just to get the chance to spend the evening at Snakes & Lattes. Clearly Snakes & Lattes is working wonders for the surrounding businesses as well as for its customers.

While you can get great coffee and food at Snakes & Lattes, the value the café delivers isn't a full stomach at the end of the evening; it's in the connection the customers make over the games. It's in the unique experience customers have and the emotional connection to each other and to times past.

100% HONEST

When Josh Bahen bit into his first real bar of chocolate while working in the wine business in France, he wondered why he'd never tasted anything like it back home in Australia. As a winemaker, he understood that the flavour was a direct result of the quality of ingredients used. He knew that how a producer treated those ingredients during the journey from raw material to end product determined the taste. Working in the high-end wine business had taught Josh the importance of not compromising on quality at any point in the manufacturing process.

Back home on the family farm in Margaret River, Josh began to research chocolate production inside and out. He wanted to understand how a product dating back centuries became unrecognizable from the original during the industrial era. Josh didn't have to dig too deeply. The world's cacao bean supply had been affected by the need to grow trees for disease resistance and yield, rather than for the quality of the beans. Josh decided that he wanted to change that and take chocolate making back to its Mayan and Aztec roots by making chocolate in its purest form.

Josh reclaimed traditional chocolate-making machinery from Europe and set up a factory to make stoneground chocolate on the farm in Margaret River. He sources beans directly from cacao bean farmers in Brazil, Madagascar, and Papua New Guinea ("Direct Trade" means that no middleman is required and all of the profits go to farmers). He is also working with farmers in Papua New Guinea, Solomon Islands, and Vanuatu, helping them to improve the quality of their beans during harvesting so that he can make "single-origin bars from areas which have never had their own unique bars."

Josh and his wife, Jacq, launched Bahen & Co. in 2011. Bahen handcrafts every bar of chocolate, using just two ingredients: cacao beans and cane sugar. The beans are sourced from a handful of farmers whom Josh has looked in the eye. The beans are ground at the factory using vintage machinery. The flavour is determined by the origin and type of bean used, not by adding artificial ingredients. The bars are wrapped and packed by hand. Josh and Jacq are building their brand with 100% honesty, not just in the raw materials and manufacture of their product, but in their ethics. Bahen & Co. pays multiples of the World Trade price to its growers.

Customers who buy a $10 bar of Bahen chocolate are buying much more than a product. They are buying into the intention and integrity with which the chocolate was made, and that changes the value of everything.

QUESTIONS FOR YOU

What are you really selling?
Are you delivering joy or promising safety and security? What's
the benefit or maybe the shortcut you deliver to your customer?
Is it convenience, more time, or something else?

How are you least like the competition?
Snakes & Lattes customers come for something more than the
coffee. Josh makes chocolate without compromises.

Why would customers cross the street to buy from you?
Have you given them a good enough reason?

**How does opening and using your product or experiencing
your service make your customers feel?**
Do you know? Have you asked? Have you ever heard someone
rave about unboxing a computer or a phone? If you have, I bet it
was an Apple product.

Name and tagline—
Your opening move

"A brand name is more than a word. It is the beginning of a conversation."
—LEXICON BRANDING, INC., WEBSITE

Naming your business is every bit as hard as naming your baby, except that you've got the added problem of securing the domain name. As I wrote in *Make Your Idea Matter*, your business or product name is the hook upon which you hang your story and start the conversation with your customers. Your brand and product names can become priceless assets. A brand name should make you stand out, not blend in.

Brand names are not just identifiers; they really can take a business or idea in one direction or another. The best brand names and taglines amplify what's great about a company. They can be designed to build mystery, can form the basis of a movement, and can even help to build cult status. A name can change how the customer feels about the product. "Italian Almond—Real Leaf Tea" just tastes better than plain old Almond Tea (believe me, I know!). The name tells a story that I want to believe and am happy to pay a little bit extra for.

A great name can take a business places that a good name can't. It makes room for a new story in peoples' hearts and minds, and it can help to position a product beyond its utility. I doubt that Zappos would have come as far with its original company name, Shoe Site. Changing to Zappos (derived from the Spanish word for shoes, *zapatos*) was clearly the right thing to do because it paved the way for the brand to diversify into other products.

Your brand name should be designed to create lofty expectations and to make people believe something, not just notice it. It should signal your difference to the world. Don't set out to name your company or product. Set out to name your vision of what you want to see in the world.

WOOHOO!

Cilla Hegarty's company, NZ Tax Refunds, has been helping New Zealanders to access their tax refunds from the Inland Revenue since 2008. Backed by the most up-to-date technology and great customer service, the company can process online applications 24/7, and in most cases customers know within sixty seconds of filling out the form whether they are due a refund and how much it will be.

Despite offering a great service, the company had a problem. The business was growing, but as more competitors came into the market, there was little or no way for a customer who was searching for this service online to differentiate one service provider from another. Many of the company's competitors had similar names and URLs (Tax Refunds, My Tax Refund, My Refund), and because of the nature of the business, a substantial number of customers searched for the service online. Even though Cilla's company had an excellent reputation, it was hard for potential customers to easily find NZ Tax Refunds in a Google search. Even when they had been recommended by another customer, it was difficult for new clients to know that they had found the right company. Regardless of the provider they used, the result for the customer was usually the same.

Cilla wanted to build on the relationships the company had with customers and differentiate her business. She wanted to make an emotional connection with her customers, generate brand loyalty, and deliver a little more joy (along with their refunded tax dollars in the bank). This wasn't just a business decision for Cilla. Her city, Christchurch, had suffered two earthquakes the previous year, and the city and its people were trying to rebuild their lives in the face of grief and uncertainty.

NZ Tax Refunds recruited a marketing agency to help them define the experience they delivered in the moment to their customers. The WooHoo campaign, complete with signature orange branding, was launched on TV, in print, and online with the URL woohoo.co.nz on April 1, 2012. What exactly is a WooHoo? As the company's website says,

"It's that moment when something unexpectedly great happens. Like when you spot a parking space that everyone else has missed. Or, when you get a big wad of cash refunded from the Inland Revenue. One part Woo. One part Hoo."

WooHoo has not only increased brand awareness (by twice as much compared to their competitors across some media channels), attracted new customers, and improved the bottom line for NZ Tax Refunds; it's also become part of the culture of the city. The company sponsors the local rugby club, The Crusaders. When the team scores, "WooHoo" appears on the screen near the ground, and the crowd joins in with the chant.

The tagline "Do you have a WooHoo waiting?" changed the conversation about what it felt like to get even a tiny and unexpected windfall.

JUST DO IT

Have you ever heard of Blue Ribbon Sports? I didn't think so.
And if you had, you probably wouldn't remember them or be
inspired by the name. Blue Ribbon officially changed its name
to Nike in the late '70s. It turns out that naming your sports
brand after the Greek goddess of victory changes everything. It
was a smart move. Today Nike is the most valuable sports brand
in the world.

A decade after the company's name change, Nike began using
the tagline "Just Do It" as an evocative and inspiring call to action in late-'80s ad campaigns. The tagline is credited with helping Nike to increase its share of the sports shoe market in the U.S.
from 18% to 43% in the first ten years after they began using it.
"Just Do It" is still working for Nike twenty-five years later.

The brand name and tagline aren't everything, of course, but no
one would deny that they are assets that Nike owns and has put
to work for the company.

QUESTIONS FOR YOU

What do you want your name to communicate about your brand?
Facts, feelings, values, advantages, or something else?

Do your name and tagline communicate your intention to staff and customers?
Or do they just fill whitespace on your business card?

How does your name differentiate your brand?
How does hearing and saying your name or tagline make customers feel?

Content and copy

*"Your company's story, product descriptions, history, personality—
these are the things that go to battle for you every day. Your words
are your frontline."*
—JASON FRIED, CO-FOUNDER, 37SIGNALS

Your content and copy are the way you woo your customers.
They are your voice and the way you communicate your brand's
personality. Content comprises the words, images, audio, and
video you use to tell people who you are, what you do, and more
importantly, how you can help them. And in an online world, it's
increasingly the way you will connect with your customers.

Many business owners are scared of sounding unprofessional, so
they professionalize their content with jargon. The result is that
they end up sounding just like their competitors. It's important
to remember who you're writing for. Jargon puts your clients
to sleep, kills the conversation dead, and sucks the soul out of
your ideas. Do your words make customers feel something, or is
your content riddled with jargon instead of being illuminated by
truth? Are you trying too hard to sound more professional, bigger, slicker, and more polished than the competition?

People have a choice nowadays; they don't have to stick around
to read your brochure or watch boring infomercials when better
content is just a click away. If nobody is going to read or watch
it, what's the point of creating it?

Think of your content and copy as being like a first date. It's the
way your brand starts establishing the kind of relationship that

leaves people wanting more. Your content doesn't need to give all of the facts; it simply needs to foster the next conversation with a customer.

THE BEST CONFIRMATION EMAIL EVER WRITTEN

When Derek Sivers first built his business CDbaby.com, he set up a standard confirmation email to let customers know their order had been shipped. After a few months, Derek felt that this email wasn't aligned with his mission—to make people smile. So he sat down and wrote a better one.

Your CD has been gently taken from our CD Baby shelves with sterilized contamination-free gloves and placed on a satin pillow.

A team of 50 employees inspected your CD and polished it to make sure it was in the best possible condition before mailing.

Our packing specialist from Japan lit a candle and a hush fell over the crowd as he put your CD into the finest gold-lined box that money can buy.

We all had a wonderful celebration afterwards and the whole party marched down the street to the post office where the entire town of Portland waved "Bon Voyage!" to your package, on its way to you, in our private CD Baby jet on this day, Friday, June 6th.

I hope you had a wonderful time shopping at CD Baby. We sure did. Your picture is on our wall as "Customer of the Year." We're all exhausted but can't wait for you to come back to CDBABY.COM!!

—Derek Sivers, Anything You Want

The result wasn't just delighted customers. That one email brought thousands of new customers to CD Baby. The people who got it couldn't help sharing it with their friends. Try Googling "private CD Baby jet"; you'll find over 900,000 search results to date. Derek's email has been cited by business blogs the world over as an example of how to authentically put your words to work for your business.

> *"When you're thinking of how to make your business bigger, it's tempting to try to think all the big thoughts and come up with world-changing massive-action plans. But please know that it's often the tiny details that really thrill people enough to make them tell all their friends about you."*
> —Derek Sivers

TAKING THE BISCUIT

During the third quarter of the 2013 Super Bowl, disaster struck when a power outage caused some of the lights in the Superdome to go out for half an hour. Thinking on their feet, the social media marketing team for the cookie brand Oreo seized the moment and leaped into action.

They posted a message on Twitter. "Power out? No problem." The message was accompanied by an image of a dimly lit Oreo cookie with a caption that read "You can still dunk in the dark."

The tweet was retweeted over 16,000 times. Advertisers had spent up to $4 million for spots during the game, and Oreo stole the show with a single timely, culturally relevant tweet—a combination of image and words, working together, posted at a time when the audience was tuned in and looking for advertisers who were working to earn their attention.

CHANGING THE CONVERSATION AND IMPROVING THE BOTTOM LINE

Old Spice, the seventy-five-year-old brand of men's grooming products, had begun to lose market share in the body wash category as the market became more and more crowded. Under the direction of the digital agency Wieden+Kennedy, the brand's manufacturer, Procter & Gamble, aimed to change how women (who were buying more than half of the body wash products) felt about their men wearing "lady-scented body wash."

The video campaign called "The Man Your Man Could Smell Like," starring Isaiah Mustafa, was launched online in July 2010 during Super Bowl weekend. On the first day, the campaign received almost 6 million views. After the first week, Old Spice had 40 million views. Traffic to their website was up 300% and Facebook fan interaction was up 800%. Within six months, the campaign generated 1.4 billion impressions.

In the six months after the campaign launched, sales of Old Spice increased by 27% over the previous year. Within a year, sales were up 107%. What made this campaign so successful was the way it poked fun at the masculine stereotype. Of course, using an actor who scored an 11 for attractiveness on a scale of 1–10 didn't hurt, either. Fans of the original YouTube video began posting parodies, which heightened interest in the original content and helped to anchor the brand in the minds of a younger audience. I remember Old Spice being the aftershave my seventy-something Dad got for Christmas in a gift set, along with soap on a rope. This ad campaign changed the set of meanings that people like me and a whole generation had attached to the brand.

QUESTIONS FOR YOU

Could you remove the logo from your website or marketing materials and substitute it with a competitor's logo?
Could they use yours?

Do you write like you speak?
Is there a single word on your website that you wouldn't use in conversation?

Does your customer recognize your brand voice?
How do you differentiate from your competitors in your copy?

How does reading your website copy and your marketing materials, or watching and listening to your video and audio, make your customers feel?
How do you want them to feel? Are you creating content that achieves that?

Design

In business, design usually does two things. It serves as the visual shorthand that helps people to make decisions about your brand: colour, typography, packaging, architecture, uniforms, store layouts, and on and on. It also shapes the user's experience of your products and—if it's good design—makes them work better. Design is your brand's fingerprint—the outward sign of your DNA.

Design can make ideas tangible, elevate the value of a commodity beyond its function, and make something more desirable by changing how people feel. Store layouts and packaging design can change how much people spend in the moment.

Design can be your brand's signature. Think about how Apple made white devices and ear buds cool when every other company was using black. Design makes shoes with shiny red soles more valuable than ones without.

NOT JUST SHINY

Christian Louboutin's signature shiny red-soled shoes are such a huge part of how he communicates his brand story that the luxury-shoes designer filed a trademark infringement suit against designer Yves Saint Laurent in 2011, seeking $1 million in damages. In September 2012, the court ruled that Louboutin retains the exclusive right to use the colour red on the bottom of its shoes whenever the outer portion of the shoe is any colour besides red.

You can't buy a pair of Louboutin's for less than $500, and a custom-made pair will cost you upwards of $4,000. Signature design, then, is not just decorative; it's a differentiator and a waymarker for customers. It also changes how a woman feels when she wears those shoes.

Of course, anyone could have made the functional part of the shoe, the thing that nobody was paying attention to, red or green with pink polka dots for that matter. The point is that they didn't. Louboutin took the thing that everyone was ignoring, gave it meaning, and made it the reason that women would cross the street and continents to buy their shoes from him. Louboutin was inspired by a notice he had read years earlier, forbidding women to wear stilettos into a museum for fear of damaging the wooden floor. "I wanted to defy that. I wanted to create something that broke rules and made women feel confident and empowered." True to his purpose, he made women feel sexier and more beautiful and gave them a story to tell without having to say a word.

GARBAGE OR ART?

Back in 2001, Justin Gignac was working as a design intern at MTV in New York. He became incensed one day when someone made a throwaway remark about how packaging design didn't matter. Justin set out to prove the doubters wrong.

Staring out of the office window onto the street below, he wondered what product he could design packaging for to make it more valuable. The overflowing trashcans were his inspiration. Weeks later, Justin went out onto the city streets, donned his gloves, and set to work picking through garbage. He took the garbage back to his apartment, sealed it in a Perspex box, signed and dated each one, and added a little touch of branding design magic on the label, which read, "Garbage of New York City. 100% authentic. HAND-PICKED from the fertile streets of NY, NY."

As a student, Justin was supplementing his income, so he decided to set up shop on a cardboard box in New York City, and he sat for half a day trying to sell one of his garbage cubes for $10. Just as he was about to give up, a customer who spoke very little English but seemed to "get it" bought one. And over time the idea caught on. To curb demand, Justin raised his prices, and still the cubes kept selling. Eventually he raised prices again and began charging $50 for his garbage cubes. Justin has created special-edition $100 cubes for events such as President Obama's inauguration, and he was commissioned to create garbage cubes for the St. Patrick's Day parade in Dublin.

Justin says that when he was charging $10 for the cubes, people thought they were a bit of a joke. When they were priced at $25, they were cool, quirky NYC souvenirs, but when the price rose to $50, people believed they were art. Justin effectively used design to add meaning to something that was worthless in any other context, changing how people felt about a previously useless item.

QUESTIONS FOR YOU

What does your design (colours, logo, packaging) communicate about your brand?
A sense of fun, professionalism, or…?

How does the way you use design differentiate you from your competitors?
Jimmy's Iced Coffee uses design to help their products stand out in the boring milk fridge in supermarkets. What does your design do?

How are you using design as an asset?
NZ Tax Refunds uses the colour orange in all its marketing. Virgin Atlantic differentiated its brand in the '80s with red shoes for female cabin crew.

How does experiencing the design of your products, branding, website, and so on make your customers feel?
Colour can change how people feel about your company, create a sense of fun, or help build trust.

Your actions

These are probably labelled "processes and procedures" in the manual that lives in a dusty A4 folder on the top shelf of your office. How you do everything, from greeting customers to answering the phone and requesting payment, is part of your story. Your actions are your customer support, the kind of service you provide, and the systems you have in place to support that. Eye contact, smiles, patience, empathy, wait times, reservation systems, apologies, and the intention with which you carry them out give customers a reason to believe you or not.

It should go without saying that your actions must be aligned with your company values.

Making a difference to your customers can be as simple as the way you sign off your emails or as complex as fire safety precautions at a rock concert. How you act—and the system you have in place to make sure that happens consistently—forms the basis of what customers will come to expect from you.

TWO BOLD IDEAS

When Scott Harrison founded charity: water, he wanted to address one of the most frequently asked questions from donors to any charity or cause. "How much of the money I donate actually goes to fund the projects directly?" And he wanted to be able to give the same transparent answer to them every time. Scott had the bold idea of having two separate accounts, one for donations made to water projects and one for expenses. Charity: water pledged to use 100% of public donations for water projects and to find another way to cover operational costs, along with the reimbursement of credit card fees charged when donations were made online. Charity: water depends on private donors and sponsorship to cover all their operating costs, from staff salaries to office rent. This new transparent 100% model was groundbreaking in the non-profit sector, and the simplicity and transparency of it have made it easier for donors to get on board.

Charity: water also wanted to close the loop between donors giving the money and their understanding of its impact. The organization does this by tracking dollars raised and showing donors how and where their money helped to make a difference. Using GPS and photos taken by their partners in the field, charity: water shows donors the exact communities their dollars helped.

These two operational procedures enable charity: water to tell one of the most transparent stories in the non-profit sector. They have found ways to engage their donors more fully and to demonstrate their commitment to their vision and values in their operations.

THREE TRUE STORIES

To all of Arthur's family,

We were so sorry that everything ended up so badly for you all last week.

It is so difficult when owners are prepared to do anything to cure their pet's problem and it's still not possible. Thank you for allowing us to try.

He was part of your lives for a short time but it's amazing how quickly they become part of the family. You are sure to be missing him terribly; we can only hope that each day gets a little bit easier.

Regards
Damian, Paul, Joanna, Rob, Nicole, Jane, Jo, Kris, Amy and all at the vets.

———

To the Ryan family,

Just a short note to express our deepest sympathy over your loss of Wilbur. It takes a pretty amazing dog to make it to 19. I think his attitude and tenacity helped him to get there. We hope you have lots of happy memories of Wilbur; as part of your family he will be deeply missed.

Yours Sincerely
Kristen, Garry, Edgar and everyone at the vets.

———

One of my dear friends was diagnosed with cancer at the beginning of a beautiful week in March. She had five biopsies taken that Friday and was sent home to wait until Tuesday or Wednesday. Her husband and three sons held their breath for four days.

Tuesday came and went. Nobody called. It's okay that they didn't have the results. It's not okay that they didn't care enough to make time to call and say, "No news yet. Are you okay? Hang in there."

Each of us has the opportunity to touch someone every single day. To really see people. To add meaning. To care. I'm not sure we do it often enough.

You might not be able to change the outcome, but you can change how people feel in a heartbeat.

How you act tells us who you are.

QUESTIONS FOR YOU

How do your actions (processes and procedures) reinforce your purpose, your vision and values?

Charity: water invests in GPS technology to show donors exactly how and where their money is being spent. This, along with their 100% model, reinforces the charity's values about transparency and accountability to donors.

How would you feel if you experienced your customer support, intake forms, call centre, or email?

Take a step back and try standing in your customers' shoes. A Genius at the Apple store recently told me that new hires get twice as much training in changing how the customer feels as they do in solving tech problems.

How do your actions make your customers feel?

MailChimp delights millions of customers with great customer service brought about by the company's creative culture.

Customer experience

"No amount of marketing will change an experience."
—Brian Solis

Customer experience is everything that happens when people encounter your brand. And whether it's online or offline, you get to design it. Most people don't put money on the table and hope that they hate the results of their choice. They actually want to fall in love with you and your brand. It's your job to give them a reason to.

The feeling your customer leaves with, as she walks out the door or clicks away from your website, is your best opportunity to differentiate your brand. Commodities are just stuff with a fixed value—until they're not. The brands you love and talk about are not the ones that competed on price or features. They are the ones that changed how it felt to buy a cup of coffee, slip on a pair of shoes, or open a laptop in a café.

THE CUSTOMERS YOU DESERVE

I was horrified to read a story which was reported in a local newspaper recently. You've probably heard a version of the story before. It goes something like this: A customer leaves the restaurant a little disgruntled after a Friday-evening dinner. The service had been particularly slow, his table had waited an hour for their meal, and the wait staff hadn't nipped his complaint in the bud. His next move is to contact the owner to give his feedback. The owner's response:

"If you wanted fast food you should have gone to McDonald's" and "I don't need you or want you to come back."

When the customer shared his story online and the reporter came knocking, the restaurant owner told her that the complaint was representative of a trend in people expecting too much from restaurants.

"We're in the business to make money, we're not there just to be a convenience to people who want to eat out," he said.

In a city where café culture is thriving, this posture could be one of the reasons this owner has to fill his restaurant with people who have bought a discount deal from a group buying website.

The flip side for him and the takeaway for you: You have the opportunity to tell the story of your business to the people you want to hear it. You get to shape the kind of brand you'd like to become. You can build your business for the customers you really want to serve.

But your customer's experience is part of that story, and customers have a hand in creating the ending. If your story sends the good ones away, you'll get the customers you deserve.

VELVET ROPES

It's Saturday afternoon and the place is packed. There is an orderly queue of grown men and women standing behind velvet ropes, waiting in line to be served, to ponder and choose. Customers, some of whom haven't been indoctrinated into the club yet, brush past the ropes to finger strategically lit designer merchandise on glass shelves set against the red walls. The smell of fresh coffee and the sound of customers on their espresso high is the first clue that you're about to walk into a specialty coffee store and not a high-end diamond boutique.

Nespresso has made the buying of their single-portion espresso capsules (for home use) a ritual. The stores, designed in the art deco tradition by French designer Francis Krempp, are called boutiques. A mix of wood, leather, glass, metal, and lighting helps create what Nespresso calls "a retail experience to satisfy your every desire." The Coffee Specialists are available to help you choose from the variety of espresso flavours on offer, including limited-edition capsules.

> *"Walking into the Nespresso store was like walking into the first-class lounge at the airport or into some secret club; it was quite exciting. Its store matches its sleek, minimal design. There is a member of staff waiting to greet you at the door and unlike a grumpy bag checker at some chain store, it was an elegant offer of assistance."*
> —STEPHANIE H ON YELP.COM

Nespresso understands who their customer is and is pulling out all the stops to change how she feels at every stage of her journey in the coffee buying experience. Nespresso has built their whole business model around the customer experience, elevating their coffee beyond a commodity.

THE BILLION-DOLLAR USER EXPERIENCE

Instagram arrived onto the saturated market that was the photo-sharing app scene in October 2010. The new kid on the block promptly shot past all of its competitors by delivering a better user experience. Instagram's differentiator was the combination of ease of use, simplicity, design, and most important, the potential for users to build an audience of their own. The founders, Kevin Systrom and Mike Krieger, refined the app so that it required as few actions as possible to post a beautiful image. Anyone with a smart phone could now make their photos (and their life) look more spectacular. Users seamlessly created something beautiful, shared it in sixty seconds, and got instant feedback, love, and adoration from an audience they built according to how good or interesting their photo stream was.

Kevin and Mike didn't have to tell the story. They gave the users a reason to do it for them and to share it with their friends. The story was baked into the interface. And the users just kept coming because their friends were there, too.

In April 2012, just eighteen months after Instagram's launch, Facebook acquired Instagram for a billion dollars in cash and stock.

QUESTIONS FOR YOU

What kind of experience do you want to deliver to your customers?

Starbucks wanted to bring the Italian coffee-drinking ritual to customers in the USA and around the world. How do you want to stand out by offering a better experience to your customers?

What's the experience they want to have in every interaction with your brand?

Can you craft an experience around how your customers want to feel? Do they want to be delighted, nurtured, listened to, pampered, or something else?

How are you going to get them there?

How does your customer experience differentiate you from your competitors? Instagram's simplicity and the fact that social sharing was built into the user interface offered users a different level of engagement with the app than that provided by other photo-sharing apps.

How does experiencing your brand, from the first point of contact to the last, make your customers feel?

How could you make that experience something that your customers can't wait to share? Dollar Shave Club customers feel savvy and they want to share the discovery of the secret with their friends.

Price and quality

When Starbucks entered the coffee market, they were having a different conversation about the price of quality than Dunkin' Donuts was. Price was one of the ways they sent a signal to customers that they were different. Price and quality are immediate signals to your customers, or at least they should be.

You can use pricing and quality to attract the type of clients you want. The price you charge sends a signal to the right people.

The summer of 1980 was a terrible time to own a hair salon on Sydney's Queen Street. The mile-long suburban street had over twenty salons to choose from, and haircuts that were once $20 had been steadily knocked down, a dollar at a time, by each salon in turn. The first salon to discount started doing cuts for $19, and very quickly every salon on the street was advertising $12 haircuts just to compete and stay open.

The situation was desperate, and many businesses were going to the wall for want of a better solution. The exception was one smart salon owner who created a big sign to put in his window, which simply read: "We fix $12 haircuts."

You don't have to tell the same story as everyone else. You actually get to choose.

And the flip side is that narrative, the stories behind objects themselves, can change their value because they attach meaning to the things. That idea is often a hard one to swallow, but Rob Walker and Josh Glenn proved it to be true, as you'll see next.

A STORY OF SIGNIFICANCE

"Stories are such a powerful driver of emotional value that their effect on any given object's subjective value can actually be measured objectively."
—JOSHUA GLENN AND ROB WALKER

In 2009, Rob and Josh set out to prove this hypothesis with the Significant Objects project. The idea was simple. They bought various objects for a few dollars at garage sales and second-hand stores. Each object was paired with a writer who wrote a fictional story about the object, giving it meaning and significance. The objects were listed on eBay, along with the stories (it was made plain to potential buyers that the stories were not true). The winning bidder got the object and a printout of the story, while the writer was given the net profit and retained the rights to the story. Rob and Josh sold $128.74 worth of cast-offs for $3,612.51 and went on to raise money for charity with phase two of the project.

THE SIX-FIGURE HAT

"Building the story creates value and ultimately can drive commerce. Stories are the foundation for what we do every day."
—*Richelle Parham, VP & CMO of eBay North America*

When Britain's Princess Beatrice stepped out in her Philip Treacy "antler hat" at her cousin William's wedding, she had no idea that it would cause such a stir or end up with its own Facebook page. She decided to put both the attention and the hat to good use by listing it for sale by auction on eBay in aid of UNICEF and Children in Crisis. The hat sold for £81,101 ($131,648).

Was the buyer buying silk and ribbon or buying the story?

"WHY DO GLASSES COST AS MUCH AS AN IPHONE?"

As Neil Blumenthal, Andrew Hunt, Jeffrey Raider, and David Gilboa began to explore the reasons glasses cost so much, they uncovered a few interesting facts. The four friends discovered, for instance, that the eyewear industry was worth $65 billion a year globally and $22 billion in the U.S. alone. And less than 1% of that business was conducted online. They also discovered that a couple of big corporations owned several sectors of the industry, from designer eyeglass brands to vision insurance providers. This oligopoly kept prices inflated.

To solve this problem, they launched Warby Parker, a company that sells high-quality prescription glasses online, with prices starting at $95. Their mission is to "create boutique-quality, classically crafted eyewear at a revolutionary price point" by creating a new business model that cuts out the middleman—something that the big established eyewear brands aren't prepared to or don't have to do. The pricing, combined with vintage-inspired design and quality, is the brand's key differentiator. And for every pair of glasses sold, Warby Parker donates a pair to someone in need. The company has married great design with good value and an even better story.

As co-CEO and founder Neil Blumenthal pointed out in his talk at PSFK 2013, this story has everything you'd want in a memorable narrative: a personal story, a "pain point," a solution, a "bad guy" (the oligopoly), and a big goal. Neil said, "Once we had that narrative, we were able to tell the world, go to GQ, go to Vogue. Everybody ... wanted to learn more about this story."

Warby Parker launched in February 2010 with "two well-placed editorials in *Vogue* and *GQ*" and a marketing budget of zero. The company hit its first year's sales targets in three weeks. They sold out of their top fifteen styles in just four weeks and had a waitlist of 20,000 customers. The company grew by 500% in a year, with sales driven primarily by word of mouth. In 2012 they gave away more than 250,000 pairs of glasses to people in need.

The company continues to thrive because of its great brand story and the loyalty that story has enabled them to build with customers. When Warby Parker opened their flagship store in New York City in April 2013, customers waited in line for up to two hours just to get into the store.

What's interesting about Warby Parker's model of delivering a competitively priced, high-quality product to customers is how this has enabled the company to disrupt the eyewear industry.

The secret to disruptive innovations and business models isn't that they disrupt the industry; it's that they disrupt people. They change how people feel about something enough to change how they behave. The average customer who needs glasses buys a pair every 2.1 years. Warby Parker set out to make glasses something that customers would buy in multiples as fashion statements, much like women buy shoes and handbags. Warby Parker wanted customers to view glasses as accessories that they could change to match occasions or moods. And while price combined with quality enables the company to tell a different story than other retailers, what changes everything is the story the customer now tells himself about how many pairs of glasses he can own and how often he should buy new ones. Many of Warby Parker's customers buy six or seven pairs of glasses at a time and not just when their prescription expires.

In his talk at PSFK 2013, Neil Blumenthal remarked, "When I look back to why we have had so much success over the last three years, it really is that we try and tell stories, because that's how humans relate to one another." Warby Parker has succeeded by giving customers a new story they can believe in.

PEOPLE WILL KNOW

How did a young yogurt company compete with industry giants who had twenty times their budget and controlled two-thirds of the market? In five years, Chobani has gone from having almost no revenue to selling a predicted $1 billion worth of yogurt in 2013.

The secret to the brand's success, according to founder and CEO Hamdi Ulukaya, is a "focus on the one cup of yogurt." He and his "Yogurt Master" spent 18 months perfecting the recipe. They focused on the quality of the yogurt and the packaging. The packaging became almost as important as the yogurt itself because without an advertising budget, the company needed to find a way for the brand to stand out in the refrigerator next to more well-known brands.

Chobani uses a shallow and wide European-style cup design that cost the company $250,000 (half of their working capital at the time). The yogurt has no preservatives and no artificial flavours (apparently that's unusual!).

> *"When it's authentic, when it's real, you don't have to say much about it. People will know."*
> —Hamdi Ulukaya, founder, president, and CEO
> of Chobani

The tiny company that opened in an abandoned Kraft factory has gone from five employees in 2005 to becoming the best-selling yogurt brand in America.

QUESTIONS FOR YOU

What's your customer's perception of the value you deliver?
Starbucks customers pay more for the unique set of meanings
that they have attached to "the Starbucks experience." They are
not just buying coffee.

What do you want to communicate with your pricing strategy?
Are you telling a story about luxury, like Jimmy Choo, or about
affordability or something else?

**How does your pricing strategy position your brand in the
hearts and minds of your customers?**
Chobani isn't the cheapest yogurt in the supermarket. The company doesn't compete on price but differentiates from its competitors on quality.

**Can your mode of service delivery, specifications, or design
add value?**
Amazon's one-click ordering offer saves customers' time. Zappos' free delivery and 365-day returns policy gives customers
peace of mind.

**How does the price they pay for the quality they receive
make your customers feel?**
Bahen & Co. customers are happy to pay more for handmade
chocolate that uses high-quality beans.

~~Position~~ Perception

Cyber Monday is fast becoming the biggest shopping day of the year. The concept was conceived by the U.S. Marketing Federation in 2005 to encourage consumers to shop online. It worked!

Many online retailers give discounts and offer promotions on the Monday after the U.S. Thanksgiving holiday, and so the shoppers come out in droves. But back in November 2011, the environmentally conscious clothing retailer Patagonia did something counterintuitive by taking out a full-page advert in the *New York Times,* encouraging people to think hard before they chose to consume. The "Don't buy this jacket" campaign highlighted the environmental impact of people's purchasing decisions and encouraged shoppers to think about reusing, recycling, and repairing. This was the act of a brand taking a stand and putting its values front and centre to help shape how they are perceived by their customers.

For decades, companies have worked on the premise that if they can dominate or be first to a market, then they win. The idea was to be the brand that was uppermost in the consumer's mind; then success, sustained growth, and profits would follow. As we've seen, even a brand as big as Pampers, which dominated mindshare and market share, couldn't keep winning by just being top-of-mind.

In 1981, Al Ries and Jack Trout described positioning as "the battle for your mind." They said, "The basic approach of positioning is not to create something new and different, but to manipulate what's already up there in the mind." Positioning

was a way to help prevent your message from being lost. To find
an easy way into a consumer's mind. To be first or to dominate
a category. A position didn't have to be what you were in *fact*.
It was what you could convince the customer to *imagine* you
were with TV ads, billboards, and jingles. Positioning was about
changing what people think and being top-of-mind. That was a
lot easier for brands to do a few decades ago in a world of limited media and limited choices.

In a Googlized world full of informed and empowered consumers, a big advertising budget is not enough to make people believe you. Your brand is no longer what you say it is. It is what
your customers feel, what they believe, and what they say as a result. It's the story as seen through their eyes, not as it is told with
advertisements and shelf space. Your position is your customers'
perception. It's shaped by the way in which you touch their
hearts, not by how you manipulate their thinking. Influencing
how your customers perceive your brand is about changing how
they feel in every interaction. If you want your customers to feel
a certain way, you're going to have to work hard to get them
there. A tagline on your packaging doesn't cut it anymore.

The good news is that what your customer believes and then
shares can build loyalty and advocacy that add enormous value
to your brand. Customers' beliefs drive all kinds of profitable
niches in every market. It turns out that being close-to-heart can
be a winning strategy.

THE GOOD LIFE

Enrico Piaggio, the son of an aircraft manufacturer, had a vision.
He wanted to help motorize the post-war Italian population
by creating a simple low-cost vehicle. Enrico had no idea what

this vision would become. His plan was to create an affordable, accessible product for the masses. That's how the Vespa was positioned when it first went on sale in Rome in 1946.

What Vespa became in the hearts and minds of the consumer, however, was a style statement. It was a symbol of freedom and all that was great about Italian style. By the time Audrey Hepburn and Gregory Peck were seen riding one in the 1950s film *Roman Holiday*, the world had begun to associate the Vespa brand with *la dolce vita* (the good life) and the joy of riding uninhibited with the wind in your hair.

A decade later, the mod subculture in Britain adopted Vespa and Lambretta scooters as its mode of transport. To these people, the Vespa was a style statement that helped them to feel like they could escape their own working-class roots. They treated the Vespa not just as a means of transportation but also as an accessory, customizing their scooters with multiple mirrors and as much chrome as possible.

Today Vespa riders, the Vespisti, celebrate their affinity to the brand and each other by joining clubs in all corners of the globe. They even have their own Vespa World Day.

More than sixty years after Piaggio launched his utility motorcycle, the Vespa brand has become an icon.

"Your Vespa will gift you with stories; you will be stopped on the streets."
—SEAN GREANEY

This wasn't the story Enrico set out to tell. It was the one his customers wanted to believe.

THE BLUE BOX

Business was booming for Tiffany & Co. in the late 1990s, thanks to the introduction of a new affordable silver jewellery line. The $110 silver charm bracelet inscribed with the Tiffany name was coveted by teenage girls, causing sales of the new silver product line to skyrocket 67% between 1997 and 2002. By 2003, company earnings had doubled and the silver jewellery line accounted for a third of Tiffany's U.S. sales.

And yet the queues of excited girls didn't fill the store managers with joy. Sure, sales were up and stores were busy, but the people close to the brand, who understood its heritage, began to worry that this lower price point would forever change how the brand was perceived by its high-end customers.

"We didn't want the brand to be defined by any single product."
—MICHAEL KOWALSKI, CEO, TIFFANY & Co.

Despite some unease from investors, Tiffany raised prices on their most popular silver products by 30% over the next three years and managed to halt the growth of their highly profitable silver line. And so the company sacrificed short-term gain and profits for the long-term good of the brand by telling the story they wanted customers to believe—that Tiffany's represents something special.

A client recently told me about her friend's excited engagement announcement on Facebook. All she did was post a photo of the Tiffany blue box—not a picture of the ring in sight. The box alone was enough to say everything she wanted to say.

QUESTIONS FOR YOU

How are you least like the competition?
Patagonia differentiates from its competitors by living their sustainable brand values in everything they do.

What do your customers believe about your brand?
Vespa is a symbol of freedom. What associations do your customers attach to your brand?

What would you like your customers to believe about your brand?
Do you want your brand to be seen as accessible or aspirational? Something for everyone or a product for a select few? More Kmart than Tiffany? How will you achieve that?

How are you changing how customers feel?
Patagonia makes their customers feel good about their conscious-consumption purchasing decisions.

Distribution

Nothing illustrates the importance of distribution as well as the demise of the Borders Bookstore chain in 2011. A forty-year business legacy was wiped out by moving too slowly to deliver what customers wanted in the way they wanted to consume it. Borders was slow to develop an online store, taking a full three years to catch up after Amazon launched in 1995. They also relied heavily on sales of CDs and DVDs at a time when music was clearly heading in the direction of digital. Borders differentiated itself by carrying a huge selection of titles (140,000 on average). But what the company thought gave them a competitive advantage was something that customers either didn't notice or didn't care about.

When they first started out in the '70s, Borders had the cozy, intimate feel of an independent bookstore, with a focus on a great customer experience delivered by knowledgeable, well-trained staff. Expansion and the opening of enormous 25,000 sq. ft. "concept stores," sometimes in out-of-town locations, changed the book-buying experience—and not in a way that customers liked.

It turns out that how you get your products and services into the hands of customers doesn't just send them a signal about your brand. When done right, distribution can also be a competitive advantage that affects your bottom line and the viability of your business. If you're not selling directly to customers, you are relying on others in the distribution chain, like retail stores, to help tell the story of your brand for you. Your distribution channels affect what you can charge and how much control you have over other aspects of your brand story. They can affect your business growth and how well your brand story can spread. If you are partnering with others to promote and sell your products, then you need to make sure that they understand the vision you have for your brand and the story you want to tell.

If you're selling apps in the App store, then you are bound by Apple's rules. You have to comply with the story they want you to tell. Amazon created an online platform that enabled them to reach more people with better distribution. Through the CreateSpace platform, Amazon also made it easier for authors to self-publish and distribute their books. Amazon invented the Kindle to make it easier to sell more ebooks.

The Kindle isn't just an ebook reader or a means of distribution. It's the foundation of an ecosystem. The more ebooks are published and the more people choose to forsake paper books, the more leverage Amazon will have with publishers to set prices. And because Amazon was the pioneer of digital book sales, the company now controls over 45% of their distribution.

GIVING IT ALL AWAY

For five years after graduating from university, Amanda Palmer worked as a living statue called the Eight-Foot Bride. She painted herself white and stood on a box on a Boston street and gave people a flower and eye contact in exchange for money, which they put in a hat at her feet. She says she got a perfect education for the music business while standing on that box. It taught her the art of asking.

Fast-forward to 2004 when Amanda and her band, The Dresden Dolls, were signed by a record label. When one of their studio albums sold 25,000 copies in the first few weeks, it was proclaimed a failure by the label. In the light of the label's attitude, the rigidity of their creative control, and their metrics for success, Amanda fought to break away from them and create a new model for distributing and selling her music. In April 2010, she announced on her blog that she had finally been released from her contract. The process took her almost two years, but this meant that Amanda was now free to sell and distribute her music on her own terms.

Her epiphany came when, after one of her gigs, a shamefaced fan came up to her and handed her $10 while telling her that he'd burned her CD from a friend. When this kept happening over and over again, Amanda realized that she had become the collection hat at her own gigs. This was the moment when Amanda decided she would give her music away for free online, and instead of *making* people pay for her music, she would *let* them. The music created by Amanda and her new band, The Grand Theft Orchestra, is available for free online. Anyone can take it, download it, torrent, share, or copy it for free. They can also choose to pay what they want.

When they were ready to launch their next album, the band turned to crowd-funding on Kickstarter; as Amanda says, "I fell into those thousands of connections that I'd made, and I asked my crowd to catch me." And they did. Almost 25,000 people helped the band to raise $1.2 million, making it the most funded music project on Kickstarter to date.

> *"The Internet and the content that we are freely able to share on it are taking us back. It's about a few people loving you up close and about those people being enough."*
> —AMANDA PALMER

That's Amanda's strategy, which informs her distribution model. A few people loving her up close and those people being enough. Her business is built around gathering a tribe of true fans by being generous with her work and herself and by trusting her fans to pay what they can for her art. It's a business model that requires a degree of bravery and trust in your audience. It means you have to understand who your right people are and create work for them.

> *"A lot of people are confused by the idea of no hard sticker price; they see it as an unpredictable risk. But the things I've done—the Kickstarter, the street, the doorbell—I don't see these things as risk; I see them as trust."*
> —AMANDA PALMER

This intimate distribution model is not something that's embraced by big business, but it's one that's being used increasingly by savvy entrepreneurs who have worked out ways to really know their fans.

FORGET THE MIDDLEMAN

Nespresso, the single-serve coffee capsule brand, has stormed ahead of its competitors by choosing to tell a different distribution story. Their secret was to invest heavily in a direct relationship with the customer by basing their business processes and IT infrastructure on what they call "service oriented architecture." By doing that Nespresso has managed to bypass the powerful supermarket giants. Nespresso coffee capsules are not available through retailers (other than its own boutiques), and the company collects as much information as possible about their customers by inducting them into the Nespresso Club and even going as far as registering their individual machine IDs.

The result of this direct relationship with the customer means that Nespresso can continue to create exclusivity and premium pricing for the brand. The bulk of their profit doesn't come from the coffee machines, just as Hewlett-Packard's doesn't come from the printer. It comes from the lock-in to the Nespresso capsules and brand experience.

QUESTIONS FOR YOU

How does your distribution channel respond to your customers' wants and needs?
The Iconic online store offers a three-hour delivery service within Sydney. Imagine the luxury of shopping from your desk on your Friday lunch hour and being ready to party in a new designer dress by 5:00 the same afternoon.

What problem does your mode of distribution solve for customers?
iTunes made it easy for music lovers to buy the songs they wanted without having to buy the whole album.

What value does your mode of distribution add?
Amanda Palmer empowers fans to feel more connected to her as supporters by asking and not insisting that they pay for her music.

How does the way you provide access to your goods and services make your customers feel?
To their detriment, Borders changed how people felt about shopping for books by stripping away the intimacy of the experience.

Location

We all understand the maxim "location, location, location" when it comes to investing in property. But how can location affect your brand story? It's obvious that if you're selling $1,500 Jimmy Choo shoes, you need to consider the location of your store carefully and choose a place with other upmarket shops nearby. For a business like Hiut Denim, which was born from the purpose of bringing jeans-making back to Cardigan, the location *is* the story.

Your location has to align with your business strategy. When Mark and Cindy were looking for a retail space for their bakery (see Chapter 20), they knew they wanted it to be in a neighbourhood location that was accessible by public transport and that people could walk to. The location was part of the story they wanted to tell about a local business serving a community.

The luxury British brand Burberry made strategic decisions about the location of its stores when the company switched from a wholesale to a retail sales strategy. At a time when other brands were forced to forsake the high street because of the growing trend towards online shopping, Burberry opened 105 new stores in wealthier cities like London, New York, Venice, and Beijing and in untapped emerging markets like Asia and the Middle East. The decision to expand into these locations was a deliberate attempt to attract well-off younger customers and tourists.

Urban beekeepers Vanessa Kwiatkowski and Mat Lumalasi of Rooftop Honey in Melbourne are on a mission to bring bees back to our cities. They and the businesses that support them are "part of a global effort to help save the honey bee from the various threats of disease and human habitation." So Vanessa and Mat take their services to the customer, re-homing swarms of honeybee colonies on the "unused roofs, balconies and gardens" of Melbourne businesses. The fruit of their labour, 100% raw honey, is stocked at a select number of cafés and stores around the city and is used in the cafés and restaurants housed below the rooftops where the bees are kept.

Of course if your customers are online, then that's where you must meet them. The shift in the way people buy music is an example of how customers' purchasing decisions can affect the location strategy and business model of an entire industry. Amanda Palmer works hard to meet her audience online, engaging them on her blog, her YouTube channel, and social media platforms. She no longer needs a record store to stock her CDs in order to reach her fans. Meanwhile, HMV closed 240 stores because people changed their minds about where they wanted to shop for music.

Location, though, isn't just about where you choose to do business; it's about figuring out where your customers are, and that's still important even in an online, less localized world. In fact, the sheer number of users in one place is what makes Facebook so valuable to businesses looking to capture attention. Where else is it possible to reach a billion pairs of eyeballs in one place in the post–TV-industrial complex era? You could argue that each Facebook profile is just another cookie in their store. We are Facebook's commodities, not its customers.

The most beautiful shopfront in the world is useless if your customers want the convenience of shopping and interacting with your brand online. Where you choose to interact with and sell to your customers—and, more important, where *they* want to connect with you—must form part of your story strategy.

Do you want to be on every street corner, like McDonalds, or tucked away down a hidden alleyway in a trendy city? Will you reach out to people physically or digitally, and why?

BE THE BRAND PEOPLE SEEK OUT, NOT THE ONE THEY STUMBLE UPON

Northbridge is the entertainment and restaurant district in the city of Perth. At night it's where a lot of the action happens, with clubs and restaurants opening until the small hours to cater to the Gen Y weekend crowd. Rochelle Adonis Cakes and Confections has an unassuming shopfront at the quieter end of the suburb.

Rochelle's brand began life as a "referral-based, by-appointment only business" in 2001. When she finally decided to expand seven years later, Rochelle could have chosen to open her up-market cake boutique in a prime city location where passers-by would become customers, or in any one of a dozen affluent suburbs. She decided instead to build her business across the railway line on a quiet street a couple of kilometres outside the city. Rochelle's studio is the kind of place you have to know about to find. Many Perth foodies don't even know that her studio exists, despite her business being featured in *Australian Gourmet Traveller* and on national television.

Today she sells cakes from her retail store, supplies more than fifty upmarket restaurants, and creates a unique high-tea experience for discerning customers.

Businesses like Rochelle Adonis survive on word of mouth; they continue to thrive because of scribbled introductions on the backs of napkins and rave reviews passed from one customer who was blown away to a friend she cares about. Because of its location on the fringes of Northbridge, Rochelle's studio has become a place you make time to visit on purpose. While the odd customer might wander in off the street, Rochelle's core clientele is made up of people who know that bookings for high tea are a must. The location enables Rochelle and her staff to tell the story they want to tell. It frames the brand's scarcity and adds to its mystique and to the appeal for Rochelle's target audience.

MEATBALLS AND THE RED CUSHION YOU DIDN'T NEED

A trip to IKEA has become a family outing. You pack the car, lure the kids with the promise of meatballs at the end, and head off on an expedition. The location of IKEA's stores is no accident. In order to keep prices as low as possible, IKEA builds stores in out-of-town locations which are close to major road networks. This strategy enables IKEA to save money in two ways. The land in these locations is cheaper, and the size of the stores allows products to be bought, transported, and stored in bulk.

The money IKEA saves aligns with their strategy of providing the best value to their customers. And because they are out of town, IKEA has created a complete customer experience under one roof by providing a café and childcare facilities.

The money you saved on the table and chairs was probably spent on meatballs in the café. IKEA designed it that way. Their location is part of their brand strategy and the story they tell.

QUESTIONS FOR YOU

Does the location of your business fit with the rest of your brand story?
Sounds obvious, but an upmarket boutique won't thrive in an area with high unemployment. The fact that Rochelle's studio is tucked away adds to the brand's mystique.

Where are your customers?
Where would your customers expect or need to find you? Think about their values, habits, and choices.

How does the location of your business make customers feel?
Think secret knocks, or a special day out shopping in the city with girlfriends. IKEA's locations make customers feel like they are part of an adventure. How could your location embellish your brand's story?

How does your location support the rest of your business strategy?
Burberry understands why it's opening more stores in China. Have you thought about where your business will thrive and why?

Ubiquity or scarcity

Instagram, the photo-sharing app, became the largest mobile social network in 2011 because the founders built ubiquity into the interface. The app simply worked better when you shared it with your friends. They gave their customers a story to tell.

Why is there a month-long waiting list for a table in Jamie's Italian restaurant in Perth, and how does that make the experience of eating there all the better once it finally happens? And why does my Italian Almond Tea, which I buy ten boxes at a time when I eventually find it because it's not stocked in every supermarket, feel like gold dust?

Do you want to have a product in every store, or will being selective about where your brand is stocked align with your story? Is your plan to have a presence on the tablet of every consumer with access to an Internet connection, or will you serve just a handful of consulting clients each year? Part of the strategy for TOM Organic feminine hygiene products was to make them accessible so that more women could make an informed choice. This meant that one of TOM's business goals was to be stocked in both of the major Australian supermarkets. On the other hand, stocking and selling Josh Bahen's chocolate bars alongside cheaper mainstream brands wouldn't align with the boutique nature of the product.

If you don't decide whether you are this or that at the outset, then how can you tell a story that will resonate with the people you want to believe it?

THE STORY YOU TELL IS A CHOICE

There wasn't much of a market for Greg Smallman's guitars back in 1970. At the time, he modelled them on the best Spanish-style guitars in production, but he thought he could make something better by getting feedback from classical guitarists about exactly what worked and what didn't. The trouble was that their opinions weren't consistent. So Greg decided to ask the Australian guitar legend John Williams what he should do. Armed with John's feedback, Greg went away and set to work. Two years later, he went back to John and showed him one of his two new guitars with a new, innovative, super-light soundboard. John bought it immediately and Greg's business began to grow by word of mouth amongst the classical guitarist community.

Greg now operates his tiny luthier business from Esperance, a remote town in Western Australia. His clients have to seek him out. He doesn't advertise and has no marketing strategy other than building the best guitars he can build, alongside his sons Damon and Kym, who joined the business in 1999. Smallman guitars sell for $25,000 a piece and only fourteen are made each year. Greg has a seven-year waiting list. His business model frames his scarcity. There is no capacity to build an extra guitar this year. No way to reliably increase capacity, no increase in production to satisfy demand. Greg's commitment to perfection doesn't scale. And that's a huge part of the story.

HERE COME THE SIRENS

Starbucks, the largest coffeehouse chain in the world, had just six stores in Seattle in 1986. Three years later, that number had increased to forty-six stores across the U.S. By 2012, Starbucks had more than 20,000 stores in over sixty countries worldwide and the green siren logo was one of the most well-recognized brand marks in the world. The company has even opened a store on a Royal Caribbean cruise ship. Starbucks expanded so rapidly between 1987 and 1992 that revenue went from $1.3 million to $73.5 million in just those five years. And even though Starbucks closed nearly 1,000 under-performing stores in the wake of the global financial crisis, the company is still expanding globally.

Starbucks has become so ubiquitous that when Hurricane Sandy hit the city of New York in October 2012, the weather.com website informed people that schools, subways, and Starbucks would be closed. You can't get much more ubiquitous, or more central to your customers' daily lives, than that. Well, perhaps more ubiquitous—Starbucks branches are vastly outnumbered by Dunkin' Donuts branches in NYC—but not more central. As *Quartz* reported, "Dunkin' Donuts followed suit with many (but not all) New York branches closing, but no one seemed to care."

QUESTIONS FOR YOU

Do you want to appeal to the masses or create products and services for people with a particular worldview?
Something for everyone or serving a niche?

How do you want people to find you?
Word of mouth or a double-page spread in *Vogue*?

How does your location affect other keys to your story?
Think about pricing, staffing, and more.

How does the accessibility of your brand make customers feel?
Part of the "in" crowd, special, cherished, served?

Community

Smoke signals are said to be the oldest form of visual communication. For centuries, native tribes used smoke signals as a way of sharing news, communicating danger, and announcing their arrival to a new area. The most important ideas were shared and spread because the tribe itself wanted to share them. So it was that the butchers, bakers, and candlestick makers of the last generation survived. The community shared and supported good work that mattered.

During the pre-Internet world of the TV-industrial complex, the people who owned the media channels took away our fires and our blankets (for a little while). Mass-market advertising used huge budgets to light big fires to generate signals about ideas that the community hadn't endorsed. The decision about what messages were worth broadcasting was taken from the people. The media told us which messages were important according to their agenda, not for the good of the tribe. We learned about what cereal we should eat and which car we should drive from the companies who could afford to make the biggest fires under their blankets.

Alas, in a cruel twist of fate, the Internet stole the power of their fires and blankets right from under their noses. Sure, the big companies still had the money to light bigger fires, but the customers they were signalling to had built fires of their own.

In a hyper-connected digital world, our individual influence goes way beyond the village where we live. Our smoke signals have the power to travel continents in a moment. Whatever you're building or selling, you can't do it in isolation. You need a community of people who care about what you're doing. Part of the purpose of your brand story is to bring people along with you. You need your customers to do more than just visit your store. You need them to send signals about your story out to the tribe. You need to give them a story to tell. Customers are why you are here. And they buy from you because of what an association with your brand says about them.

Jørgen Vig Knudstorp, CEO of The Lego Group, tells one of my favourite stories about the positive impact of a brand collaborating with its community. When Lego was developing a new range of medieval castle building sets, they asked a group of fans for feedback. The children in the group had just one question: "Where's the dragon?" When they were politely told by the grownups that there were no dragons during medieval times, the kids responded by saying, "What's fun about that?" I'm guessing that Lego added dragons to those sets.

"… LEGO fans, the LEGO community. They define what LEGO is all about."
—Jørgen Vig Knudstorp

Today the brands and ideas we buy into and care about are shorthand for creating meaning in our lives. Our purchases, Facebook likes, and things we choose to share with our friends are part of our personal story. They are outward signs of what matters to us.

People buy your product or share your idea because…

It makes them feel… better, smarter, more beautiful, healthier, safe, loved, and on and on.
Online courses, Jimmy Choo shoes, perfume, gym membership, life insurance, organic fruit.

They are looking for a shortcut. Information, more time, easy payments, or something else.
PayPal, lawn mowing, TripAdvisor.

They want to feel more connected to the group, to belong.
Instagram, live events, Startup weekend, book clubs.

It works.
Think Dropbox, WordPress, Amazon, FedEx.

It makes their lives easier.
Fruit smoothies, online groceries, Thermomix.

It gives them a story to tell.
A Tiffany & Co. bracelet, dinner at Jamie's Italian restaurant, Christian Louboutin red-soled shoes.

They need a solution to a problem.
Online dating, personal training, gluten-free bread.

It helps them get from where they are to where they want to be.
Gym membership, consulting services, design.

They like what you stand for.
Whole Foods Markets, Method cleaning products, Patagonia outdoor wear.

Their friends are doing it, too.
Facebook, dinner at a new restaurant, Jägerbomb cocktails.

This is why great brands become a part of the customer's story, and customers in turn help to shape the brand's story.

SHARED EXPERIENCES

From its humble beginnings in that San Francisco apartment in
2008, Airbnb has become *the* community marketplace to list or
book unique places to stay anywhere in the world. As Chapter
3 mentioned, it's possible to find a place to stay at every price
point in more than 33,000 cities and 192 countries. But what
the Airbnb founders are most proud of is the 600 million social
connections (to date) that have been made as a result of people
using the service. (Remember Brian Chesky's vision: to "connect
people … all over the world….") The website that started out
as a place to search for accommodations quickly evolved into a
social platform.

To support that evolution, the Airbnb founders recognized and
then overcame a series of limitations. Firstly, they realized that
people who weren't travelling for conferences but still needed a
place to stay might use Airbnb. Now you can book a room anywhere, anytime. Secondly, they discovered that people wanted
to rent other types of spaces. Now you can also book cars, work
and event spaces, and even a tree house or an igloo. Next, the
founders considered all of the people who didn't know where exactly they wanted to go, and wondered how Airbnb could help
them find the hidden gems—listings that weren't being discovered. Enter Wish Lists.

Airbnb did provide a way for users to highlight their favourite
properties with a star, but—as Joe Gebbia explained to Cliff
Kuang of Co.Design—when Joe's team went looking for ways to
deepen user engagement, they hit upon the idea of changing the
star to a heart. Engagement shot up by 30%. This simple tweak
shone a light on the potential to make the site about more than
accommodation searches and gave rise to a site redesign around
the creation of Wish Lists.

Users can create their own Wish Lists of dream destinations, share their lists with friends online, and see the places their friends dream of visiting. If you're planning a group holiday, you can create a shortlist to share it with the group, or you can just use your Wish List to dream. Almost half of Airbnb's users use Wish Lists.

Since the introduction of Wish Lists, people are not simply visiting Airbnb once in a while to search for accommodations; they are coming back to discover the places their friends love. Wish Lists have taken accommodation listings and transformed them into content that people care about and want to share. By adding this extra layer of meaning to the platform, Airbnb has changed the relationship people have with their service. Focusing on how the community interacted with their business enabled the team to find ways to deepen the relationship with its customers.

MOVEMBER

It started out as a simple idea (and a bit of a dare) over a few beers one Sunday afternoon in a Melbourne bar in 2003. A couple of friends were chatting about fashion statements from their '70s childhood that had or hadn't made a comeback when they hit upon the idea of bringing back the moustache (or "mo" for short in Australia). They renamed the month of November "Movember" and a group of thirty guys grew moustaches, took a fair amount of ribbing from friends, family, and strangers, and threw a big party at the end of the month. The guys had so much fun that they wanted to find a way to legitimize their efforts and celebrate their journey the following year.

Inspired by the hugely positive effect that the breast cancer awareness movement was having on early detection and treatment of the disease, the "Mo Bros" set out to raise money to help do the same for prostate cancer in men. In November 2004, those same friends banded together again and grew into a group of 450 men who committed to growing moustaches for the month and finding sponsors. The Movember campaign was born, with the tagline "Changing the face of men's health." They raised $54,000 that year and donated it to the Prostate Cancer Foundation of Australia.

By 2012, the number of participants had grown to more than a million men, spread all over the globe, and the campaign had raised over $140 million. Movember has become the biggest funder of prostate cancer research and support programs in the world.

When Adam Garone, a co-founder, was asked by journalists about Movember's celebrity ambassadors, he said that every single person who participates is a celebrity ambassador.

The act of growing the moustache gave people a reason to engage with each other and start a conversation. The genius of Movember is that those who belong—"Mo Bros"—have an outward sign of being part of the group and part of something bigger than themselves. The conversations sparked by the Movember community and those moustaches raise awareness and save lives by encouraging men to think about their health and to get screening for prostate cancer.

QUESTIONS FOR YOU

Who is your ideal customer?
Don't just think age demographic; think mindset, worldviews, and aspirations. Whom does he trust? Paint a picture, understand what's on his to-do list, tell yourself his story.

What problem does he need you to solve? What does he care about?
Do you know?

Where will you find him?
Where does he hang out online and offline? What media does he consume?

Does your brand have a purpose that brings your customers together as a community? Could it?
Rooftop Honey saves bees and connects people to locally produced food. Movember raises awareness of men's health issues and funds programs and research on prostate cancer and depression.

How do you foster feelings of advocacy, ownership, and belonging amongst customers?
Lego has a tribe of "Ambassadors" who work with the company as the representative voice of the wider Lego community. Starbucks encourages customers to "submit, share and vote" for new product ideas and innovations at http://mystarbucksidea.force.com/.

Reputation

"A brand for a company is like a reputation for a person. You earn reputation by trying to do hard things well."
—Jeff Bezos, CEO, Amazon

What's the first thing you do now before you visit a new restaurant for the first time or book a hotel room online? You probably ask a friend for a recommendation or you check out the reviews online. Now more than ever, the story your customers tell about you is a big part of your story. Word of mouth is accelerated and amplified. Trust is built digitally beyond the village. Reputations are built and lost in a moment. Opinions are no longer only shared one to one; they are broadcasted one to many, through digital channels. Those opinions live on as clues to your story.

The cleanliness of your hotel bathrooms is no longer a secret. Guests' unedited photos are displayed alongside a hotel brochure's digital glossies. TripAdvisor ratings are proudly displayed by hotels and often say more about the standards guests can expect than do other, more established star ratings systems, such as the *Forbes Travel Guide*'s ratings. Once-invisible brands and family-run hotels have had their businesses turned around by the stories their customers tell about them.

"With 50 million reviews and counting, [TripAdvisor] is shaking the travel industry to its core."
—*Nathan Labenz*

It turns out that people are more likely to trust the stories other people tell about you than to trust the well-lit Photoshopped images in your brochure. Reputation is how your idea and brand story are spread. A survey conducted by Chadwick Martin Bailey found that six in ten cruise customers said "they were less likely to book a cruise that received only one star." There is no marketing more powerful than what one person says to another to recommend your brand. "Don't waste money on expensive razors." "Nice hotel; shame about the customer service." In a world where online reputation can increase a hotel's occupancy and revenue, trust has become a marketing metric.

> *"[R]eputation has a real-world value."*
> —RACHEL BOTSMAN

When we were looking to book a quiet, off-the-beaten-track hotel in Bali, the first place we looked wasn't with the travel agents or booking.com. I jumped online and found that one of the area's best-rated hotels on tripadvisor.com wasn't a five-star resort but a modest family-run, three-star hotel that was punching well above its weight. This little fifteen-room hotel had more than 400 very positive reviews and had won a TripAdvisor Travellers Choice award. The reviews from the previous guests sealed the deal.

The little hotel in Ubud was perfect. The reviews didn't lie, and of course the place was fully booked with a steady stream of guests who knew where to look before taking a chance on a hotel room. Just a few years before, this $50-a-night hotel would have been buried amongst a slew of well-marketed five-star resorts. Today, thanks to a currency of trust, even tiny brands can thrive by doing the right thing and giving their customers a great story to tell.

THE WRONG STORY CAN KILL A GREAT IDEA

I'd be hard-pressed to find a better start to a brand story than the one that chronicles the birth of "the people's car," the Tata Nano. The story goes that Ratan Tata, chairman of the well-respected Tata Group, was travelling along in the pouring rain behind a family who was precariously perched on a scooter weaving in and out of traffic on the slick wet roads of Bangalore. Tata thought that surely this was a problem he and his company could solve. He wanted to bring safe, affordable transport to the poor—to design, build, and sell a family car that could replace the scooter for a price that was less than $2,500. It was a business idea born from a high ideal and coming from a man with a track record in the industry, someone with the capability to innovate, design, and produce a high-quality product.

People were captivated by the idea of what would be the world's cheapest car. The media and the world watched to see how delivering on this seemingly impossible promise might pan out. Ratan Tata did deliver on his promise when he unveiled the Nano at the New Delhi Auto Expo in 2009, six years after having the idea. The hype around the new "people's car" and the media attention it received meant that any mistakes were very public (several production challenges and safety problems were reported along the way). And while the general public seemed to be behind the idea of a new and fun Indian-led innovation, the number of Facebook likes (almost 4 million to date) didn't convert to actual sales.

It seemed that while Tata Motors was telling a story about affordability and innovating with frugal engineering (perhaps "lean engineering" might have worked better for them), the story prospective customers were hearing was one about a car that was cheap. The positioning of the car was at odds with the buying public's perception of it. In a country where a car is an aspirational purchase, the Nano became symbolic of the car to buy if you couldn't afford anything else.

Since its launch in 2009, just over 200,000 Nanos have sold. The factory has the capacity to produce 21,000 cars a month. It turns out that the modest numbers of people buying the Nano are not the scooter drivers but middle-class Indians who are looking for a second car, or a car for their parents or children. The car that was billed as a "game changer" hasn't lived up to the hype in the hearts of the people who were expected to line up and buy it in the tens of thousands. Despite winning design and innovation awards, the Nano's reputation amongst consumers—and the story they have come to believe—has been the thing that's held it back.

SHARE OF HEART

Method became one of the fastest-growing private companies in the U.S. by creating a brand story that was designed to be shared. Co-founders and friends Adam Lowry and Eric Ryan took on the challenge of creating cleaning products that "work, for you and for the planet, ones that are as easy on the eyes as they are on the nose."

Entering a market dominated by big players like P&G, the Method founders differentiated on five areas that they thought household products fell down in: results, safety, sustainability, design, and scent. While there were eco-friendly products on the market, in Adam and Eric's experience they didn't get the job done. And the conventional products that worked required people to open their windows to get rid of toxic cleaning fumes.

The two friends wanted to produce cleaning products that were green and safe, yet effective, that smelled amazing, and that were sold in packaging that they "didn't have to hide under their sinks." Adam and Eric wanted to re-invent the eco-friendly niche by creating green products that were fun, products that people couldn't help talking about. While many new customers were attracted by the curvaceous package design and great fragrance, they became brand evangelists because of the company's green credentials.

> *"Everything we do shouldn't just inspire people to be customers but [should inspire them] to be customers and then go out and talk about it."*
> —ERIC RYAN, CO-FOUNDER, METHOD

Method found ways to engage with customers, such as with their "People against dirty" community which urges customers to "clean happy." The "People against dirty" YouTube channel has over 4 million views to date, with the "clean happy" anthem being the most watched, attracting over 1.5 million views. Customers can also sign up to receive a newsletter, which will give them "exclusive deals, sneak peeks of new products, and all the behind-the-scenes scoop." Method also identified about 5,000 people who have done something to show their love for the brand and called them "cheerleaders"—people like Nathan Aaron, who wrote about Method at his blog methodlust.com for over five years.

The Method founders knew that they couldn't gain the market share of the big players in a market segment dominated by large global brands. Instead, they built a company and created products that were designed to gain share of heart and thus share of wallet.

QUESTIONS FOR YOU

What do people say when you're not in the room?
Do you know?

What would you like them to say?
What's your vision of what customers say about the difference you make in their lives?

How will you achieve that?
What posture will you need to adopt? What actions must you take?

What does one person say to another to recommend your brand?
What story are you giving them to tell?

How do your customers feel about telling their friends about your brand?
What does their loyalty to your brand allow customers to say about themselves?

Reaction and reach

The aeroplane-shaped silver cruet sets accompanying the meals of Upper Class passengers on Virgin Atlantic flights were such a hit that customers started stealing them. So many were taken that Virgin decided to make the customers' thefts part of the story by inscribing "Pinched from Virgin Atlantic" on the bottom of the sets. That particular reaction to their brand was not something that the company had anticipated, but they leveraged it and made it work to reflect their brand values, one of which is "to put the fun back into flying."

There is no more potent reminder of the power of customer reaction than lines at the Apple store in the days leading up to a new product launch. And consider the reach of billions of email messages sent every year that are signed off with "Sent from my iPhone."

The fastest-selling paperback of all time was not the best book of all time. Word of mouth, not the quality of the writing, made the erotic book *Fifty Shades of Grey* an international bestseller. Women who weren't ordinarily big readers bought the book because their friends were reading and recommending it. The reaction of readers was all the marketing the book needed.

"Market reach" was once the term used to describe the number of potential customers it was possible to target with an advertising campaign or marketing message. My definition of reach asks you to consider the people you've touched, influenced, and affected. Think of reach in this instance not merely as measuring customer numbers but as a way of measuring impact.

Reach can be a measure of how far you've come and of the difference you've made.

How you make customers feel influences how they behave towards your brand. How your customers react to your brand is a big part of the story. Their actions demonstrate how you have touched them. You can cause conversations to happen and reactions to occur, but you can't control them. You get to start the story of your brand by giving people a way to talk about it, but your customers have a say in creating the ending.

TRUE FRIENDS

Mark and Cindy Dyck's bakery started out as a passion for baking with a wood-fired oven that Mark built in their back yard and an email list of twenty close friends. Every Wednesday afternoon he sent out an email to tell them what he was making that week. Their orders needed to be in two days before baking day so he could get everything ready for Friday. And every Friday, the delighted customers bought bread from Mark's garage. The feedback from their underground customers and their love of the work was what made Mark and Cindy decide to explore the idea of doing this business for real.

If they were going to do it, they wanted to do it right. Mark set out to learn everything he could about baking great bread. The biggest challenge in the end was finding the perfect neighbourhood location that customers could walk to; after two years of searching, just as they were about to give up, Mark and Cindy finally found the right location.

Orange Boot Bakery opened in Regina, Saskatchewan, in January 2011, on a day when the temperature didn't get much above -10°C (14°F). Mark was able to send out an email that his original twenty underground customers could finally share. In the early days, Orange Boot was probably the only bakery in the history of the world that opened its doors at 11 am. Since it was just Mark and Cindy, this was the earliest they could get all the bread out each morning.

That first year, the bakery ran a competition; two lucky customers won free bread for a year and came in once a week to have their bread basket refilled. Of course the two winners were thrilled, but Mark got to thinking about how Orange Boot could share that delight and expand the reach of the competition beyond just two people. And so "True Friends" was born.

That second year, the bakery had three winners who won a week's supply of freshly baked bread. At the end of their week, the winners were charged with the task of passing the basket on to a friend, who could take it into the bakery to be filled. Mark attached a notebook to each basket so that one friend could write a note to the next. When he or she comes into the bakery, every new friend has a photo taken so that Mark can record and map the journey of each basket over a year. And so instead of having a positive impact on just two customers, Mark and Cindy's little bakery reaches 150 and beyond through the positive stories and shared generosity with their customers.

THE STORY YOUR CUSTOMERS CAN TELL THEMSELVES

The British public first fell in love with Jamie Oliver's authentic, down-to-earth personality in the late '90s when he was featured in a documentary on the River Café. Jamie became a household name because of his energetic and infectious way of inspiring people to believe that anyone can cook and eat well. In his TV shows and cookery books and on his website, he made the concept of cooking good food practical and accessible to anyone. When Jamie Oliver opened a new restaurant in Perth, it naturally caused a bit of a buzz. High-profile personalities and big brands create an air of expectation. Brands like Jamie Oliver are talked about not just because of their fame and instant recognition, but because they have meaning attached to them. And people associate Jamie with simplicity, inclusiveness, energy, and creativity.

If you're one of the first people to have the experience of eating at the new Jamie's Italian, then you've instantly got a story that you can share with your friends. The stories we tell to others (and to ourselves) are the reason that people were prepared to queue halfway down the street when Jamie's Italian opened the doors to its Perth restaurant in March of 2013. As with pre-iPhone launch lines at the Apple store, the reaction of customers frames the scarcity of the experience. When you know there's a three-month wait for a dinner booking (there is, although 50% of the restaurant is reserved for walk-ins), it feels like a win to be one of the few to have a booking. The reaction of other people makes the story better in the eyes of prospective diners. The hype and the scarcity just heighten the anticipation of the experience.

People don't go just for the food; they go for the story they can tell. Jamie told the UK press that 30,000 napkins are stolen from branches of his restaurant every month. Customers were also stealing expensive toilet flush handles until Jamie had them welded on.

The loss of the linen and toilet fittings might impact Jamie's profits, but it also helps to create the myth of the brand.

QUESTIONS FOR YOU

How would you like customers to react to your brand?
Five-star reviews, great feedback about service, or recommendations to friends? Think about how you can create opportunities to make that happen.

Are you giving customers opportunities to demonstrate loyalty to your brand?
A quarter of Starbucks' customers buy their coffee with a preloaded loyalty card.

How could you increase your reach to the right people by telling a better story?
Mark found a great way to spread the word about his bakery with "True Friends." What could you do?

The key that nobody can give you

What do Post-it Notes, Super Glue, penicillin, the pacemaker, the microwave oven, Play-Doh, Kellogg's Corn Flakes, and Viagra have in common? They were all serendipitous inventions. Happy accidents. Products that began life as one thing but, as a result of human involvement and intuition, became something else: inventions that would change the way we live. Journalist and academic Aleks Krotoski describes serendipity as "that delightful moment when totally unrelated things come together in magical ways to change the course of destiny." Serendipity, then, is something that we cannot plan for.

If Richard Branson's flight to Puerto Rico hadn't been cancelled, if he hadn't chartered a plane for $2,000 and gone on to sell seats to fellow stranded passengers for $39, would Virgin Atlantic have been born? If the lawyer and his wife who were slated to adopt Steve Jobs hadn't changed their minds and waited for a girl instead, would he have finished college and never have founded Apple? If Yahoo had accepted the offer to buy Google for a million dollars in 1997 (five years later, they offered Google $3 billion, which Google turned down), would the Internet be what it is today? If Howard Schultz had never visited Milan and fallen in love with Italian coffee-drinking culture, would there be a Starbucks experience in more than sixty cities around the world? If Bob Geldof hadn't seen Michael Buerk's TV report from Ethiopia in 1984, how many more people might have died?

If Amanda Palmer hadn't met the red-faced fan who handed her $10 at a gig, would she be inviting fans to download her music for free and earning her living by asking them to pay something if they can? If Jim Cregan hadn't stopped at that filling station in Adelaide on his road trip in Australia, would there be a Jimmy's Iced Coffee? If Aimee Marks hadn't been prompted to look more closely at the packaging for tampons because of her design assignment, would she have innocently gone on buying them for the next thirty years instead of working to bring a greener alternative to market? If Chobani founder and CEO Hamdi Ulukaya hadn't fished the advert for the old disused Kraft factory out of the bin in 2005, would there still be a "zero to a billion" challenger brand story?

There is no way to account for every eventuality in life or in business. Any project you take on will have elements of the unknown—decisions that, if made differently, would have led to other outcomes. If any one of the entrepreneurs we've read about in these pages were starting out with exactly the same resources today, their businesses wouldn't turn out the same.

I'm not sure they teach you about serendipity at business school; perhaps they should because circumstances and how you act upon them affect the way things work out. That chance meeting with just the right person who can propel your project along. A gut decision. The opportunity you decide not to take. And of course, you and your unique story, filled with experiences, memories, and conditioning from your childhood. There is no business plan that can take into account the influence of the experiences, intentions, and bravery of the person who wrote it.

> *"The truth is that each success story has a context: a unique background, employees' motivations, and many other 'surround factors' that deeply influence the outcomes."*
> —R. Gopalakrishnan, executive director, Tata Sons

There are business books that will teach you how to think like Richard Branson and how to hire the next Steve Jobs, but there's no guaranteed way to bring them and their lifetime of experiences, successes, and failures into your business. There's no roadmap that has the route to the chance meeting or one conversation that changes everything. The truth is that there is no way to build serendipity into your business plan. Nobody knows for sure how the market will react, how customers will feel, or how the story will end. Nobody has had your unique set of experiences, your relationships, your successes and failures, your hurts and your small wins, all of which contribute to this brand story you are creating. And even though someone might be armed with similar tools and tactics, nobody can build this thing quite like you can. You hold the key.

IT'S NOT HOW GOOD YOU ARE; IT'S HOW WELL YOU TELL YOUR STORY

In 2012 Procter & Gamble spent $9 billion on advertising—more than four times what they spent on research and development. And yet brands like Method and Dollar Shave Club have been able to carve out a place in the market. Big corporations might have huge budgets and a marketing department, but you've got a story.

Story doesn't discriminate. It's not dependent on a big advertising spend, a dedicated marketing department, or a celebrity endorsement. It's the universal marketing tool available to anyone.

That includes you.

People want to see you, and they want to see reflections of themselves in your brand. They want to know who you are, what you stand for, and what made you. People want to be touched by you. They want a reason to care about you and to believe in what you do. You have to give them that reason, to change how they feel, not just what they think and do. It's a mistake to assume that your marketing should change how people feel about what you sell. Your job is to change how they feel about *themselves*. The goal of business must no longer be to find more ways to say "here we are; notice us." It has to be about reaching out to the customer and saying "we see you."

The Dove "Real Beauty" campaign—launched by Unilever in 2004 following research which discovered that "only 2% of women around the world would describe themselves as beautiful"—is an example of how even big established brands are trying to stand in their customers' shoes. But the opportunity to really empathize and connect with customers is open to businesses of any size.

You don't need permission from the gatekeepers to tell your story. You have everything you need to be able to tell it. The Internet, along with access to online tools that enable you to engage, share, and spread your ideas, has levelled the playing field. You have the power to create something from nothing and to reach out to the world with it through story.

Your customers don't just want the stuff or services you sell; they want you to take them on a journey to where they would like to go. So go find a way to tell the best story you can tell to the people who care and to the ones who might need to hear it. Work out how you are least like the competition and tell that story.

Your story starts here.

Research Notes

INTRODUCTION

1. Number of companies from the original *Fortune* 500 that are still on the list, from "No Business is Too Big to Fail or Too Small to Succeed—Sobering stats on business failures," by Brian Solis, posted on his blog, 28 February 2013. <http://www.brian-solis.com/2013/02/no-business-is-too-big-to-fail-or-too-small-to-succeed-sobering-stats-on-business-failures/>

2. Steve Jobs' "Marketing is all about values" quote from the video embedded in "The 1997 Video That Explains the Marketing Genius of Steve Jobs," by Michael Learmonth. *Ad Age*, 7 October 2011. <http://adage.com/article/digital/1997-video-explains-marketing-genius-steve-jobs/230294/>

3. Apple's status as the most valuable company in history, from "Apple Now Most Valuable Company in History," Benzinga Editorial, *Forbes*. 21 August 2012. <http://www.forbes.com/sites/benzingainsights/2012/08/21/apple-now-most-valuable-company-in-history/>

4. Jason Fried quote from "Telling Your Company's Story in

Video," by Jason Fried. *Inc.* magazine, November 2011 issue. <http://www.inc.com/magazine/201111/jason-fried-on-telling-your-companys-story-on-film.html>

5. Information about the launch of Dollar Shave Club from "Lessons in Razor's-Edge Creativity from the Dollar Shave Club," by Josh Linkner. *Fast Company* magazine, 19 March 2012. <http://www.fastcompany.com/1825408/lessons-razors-edge-creativity-dollar-shave-club>

6. Information about men's attitudes about overpriced razor blades from <http://wiki.answers.com/Q/Generally_how_many_shaves_should_you_get_from_a_Gillette_Fusion_Power_razor>.

7. Gillette-brand advertising expenditure in 2010 from "P&G Reviews PR Duties for Gillette," by Alexandra Bruell. *Ad Age*, 31 August 2011. <http://adage.com/article/agency-news/p-g-reviews-pr-duties-gillette/229549/>

8. "Whoever tells the best story wins" quote from *Whoever Tells the Best Story Wins: How to Use Your Own Stories to Communicate with Power and Impact*, by Annette Simmons. (AMACOM, 2007.)

9. Quotes from Ian Schon and information about The Pen Project from Ian Schon's website, <http://ianschon.com/pen.html>, and from his Kickstarter page, <http://www.kickstarter.com/projects/894128597/the-pen-project>.

10. Richelle Parham quote from "eBay and the Future of Storytelling," eBay Inc. blog, 8 October 2012. <http://blog.ebay.com/2012/10/ebay-and-future-of-storytelling/>

11. Quote from Malär, Krohmer, *et al.* from "Emotional Brand Attachment and Brand Personality: The Relative Importance of the Actual and the Ideal Self," by Lucia Malär, Harley Krohmer, Wayne D. Hoyer, and Bettina Nyffenegger. *Journal of Marketing*, Vol. 75 (July 2011); refers to "The Ties That Bind: Measuring the Strength of Consumers' Emotional Attachments to Brands," by Matthew Thomson, Deborah J. MacInnis, and C. Whan Park. *Journal of Consumer Psychology*, Vol. 15 (2005).

CHAPTER 1: TRUTH—WHAT BUSINESS ARE YOU IN?

1. Rob Walker quote from *Buying In: The Secret Dialogue between What We Buy and Who We Are*, by Rob Walker. (Random House, 2008.)

2. Information about Jimmy's Iced Coffee, and quote from Jim

Cregan, from interview with Bernadette Jiwa on 2 April 2013.

3. Information about the turnaround of Pampers, and quotes from Jim Stengel, from *Grow: How Ideals Power Growth and Profit at the World's Greatest Companies*, by Jim Stengel. (Crown Business, 2011.) Reprinted with permission.

CHAPTER 2: PURPOSE—THE REASON YOU EXIST

1. Neil Gaiman quote from "Neil Gaiman Addresses the University of the Arts Class of 2012," 23 May 2012. <http://www.uarts.edu/neil-gaiman-keynote-address>

2. Information about the Stengel 50, and quotation, from the Stengel Study of Business Growth, <http://www.millwardbrown.com/Sites/Brand_Ideal/The_Study.aspx>, the "Top 50 Brands" page, accessed in April 2013.

3. Jørgen Vig Knudstorp quotations from interview transcript at <http://www.meettheboss.tv/Broadcast/CEO/96/The-Man-Who-Rescued-Lego/>.

4. Lego sales information from "Rebuilding Lego, Brick by Brick," by Keith Oliver, Edouard Samakh, and Peter Heckmann, *strategy+business* magazine, Autumn 2007, Issue 48.

5. Mission statement of The Lego Group from the company website, <http://aboutus.lego.com/en-us/lego-group/mission-and-vision/>.

6. "Our town is going to make jeans again" quote from the Hiut Denim website, <http://hiutdenim.co.uk/blogs/story/5156362-our-town-is-going-to-make-jeans-again>, accessed in April 2013.

7. Information about the closing of the Dewhirst company from "Final shift for Dewhirst workers," *BBC News*, 8 November 2002. <http://news.bbc.co.uk/2/hi/uk_news/wales/2420725.stm>

8. "We will have to tell our story…" quote from the Hiut Denim website, <http://hiutdenim.co.uk/blogs/story/4801552-our-user-manual>.

9. Information about Hiut's mission and retail strategy from the company website, <http://hiutdenim.co.uk/pages/faq>.

10. David Hieatt quote, "We are defined not by what we do but by why we do it…," from video accompanying the article "Challenger Type: The Missionary," by Jude Bliss, June 2012, at eatbigfish.com. <http://eatbigfish.com/type/article/the-missionary>

CHAPTER 3: VISION

1. Paul Arden quote from *It's Not How Good You Are, It's How Good You Want To Be*, by Paul Arden. (Phaidon Press Inc., 2003.)

2. Vision statement of Room to Read from "Envisioning Our Future: A Roadmap for Learning," <http://www.roomtoread. org/Document.Doc?id=220>, accessed in April 2013.

3. Brian Chesky quotations from a video produced by Shatterbox, <http://www.shatterbox.com/video/airbnb>, accessed in April 2013, and from "The Sharing Economy," a speech given by Brian Chesky at the DLD 2012 conference; video at <http:// dld-conference.com/videos/KINsjz4K_34>.

4. Joe Gebbia quote and some of the information about the beginnings of Airbnb from a video of Joe Gebbia's talk at the 2011 PSFK Conference in New York City, "Joe Gebbia: The Airbnb Story." <http://www.psfk.com/video/single?video=23275754>

5. Additional research and quotations from the Airbnb website: <https://www.airbnb.com/story> and <https://www.airbnb.com/ about>.

6. Information and quotations about how Scott Harrison came to start charity: water from a video of Scott's interview with Kevin Rose, at the organization's website, <http://www.charity-water.org/about/scotts_story.php>.

7. Vision statement for charity: water (Mo Scarpelli quote) from the organization's website, <http://support.charitywater.org/entries/20375851-What-is-charity-water-s-vision->.

CHAPTER 4: VALUES

1. Robert Fabricant quote from "Kickstarter Rescues Startups That VCs Won't Touch, But Here's What's Missing," by Robert Fabricant. <http://www.fastcodesign.com/1669698/kickstarter-rescues-startups-that-vcs-wont-touch-but-heres-whats-missing>

2. Information about materials used to produce conventional tampons, and health concerns about those materials, from "Behind the label: tampons," by Pat Thomas, *The Ecologist*, 27 November 2007 <http://www.theecologist.org/green_green_living/behind_the_label/268961/behind_the_labeltampons.html>, and from "Tampons and Asbestos, Dioxin, & Toxic Shock Syndrome," U.S. FDA website <http://www.fda.gov/MedicalDevices/Safety/AlertsandNotices/PatientAlerts/ucm070003.htm>.

3. Quotes from Aimee Marks and information about the beginnings of TOM Organic from an interview with Bernadette Jiwa in April 2013.

4. Information about Tattly Designy Temporary Tattoos and quotes from Tina Roth Eisenberg from an interview with Bernadette Jiwa on 1 April 2013.

CHAPTER 5: PRODUCTS AND SERVICES

1. Quotations and information about Nudie Juices from the Nudie Juices website, <http://www.nudie.com.au/the-whole-truth/faq/Why-hasnt-someone-made-drinks-as-good-as-nudies-before>.

2. James Ajaka quotation from "A decade of Nudie," *Food & Drink Business*, 13 February 2013. <http://www.foodanddrink-business.com.au/news/a-decade-of-nudie>

3. Information about Moleskine notebooks from Wikipedia article, <http://en.wikipedia.org/wiki/Moleskine>.

4. Seth Godin quote from Seth's blog, <http://sethgodin.type-pad.com/seths_blog/2009/12/first-organize-1000.html>.

5. Maria Sebregondi quote from "The power of brands," inter-

view with Zoe Tabary, *The Economist Intelligence Unit*, 1 October 2012, <http://www.management-thinking.org/content/power-brands>, reprinted with permission.

CHAPTER 6: YOUR PEOPLE

1. Paul Arden quote from *It's Not How Good You Are, It's How Good You Want To Be*, by Paul Arden. (Phaidon Press Inc., 2003.)

2. Lego Group sales figures from the company website, <http://aboutus.lego.com/en-us/news-room/2012/march/annual-result-2011/>, and from "Annual Report 2012: The LEGO Group" <http://cache.lego.com/r/aboutus/-/media/About%20Us/Media%20Assets%20Library/Annual%20Reports/Annual_Report_2012.pdf>.

3. Various quotations and information about Kimpton Hotels from the company website: <http://www.imkimpton.com/?page_id=6>; <http://www.kimptonhotels.com/about-us/about-us.aspx>; <http://www.kimptonhotels.com/kimpton-cares/kimpton-cares.aspx>; <http://www.imkimpton.com/?page_id=24>; <http://www.imkimpton.com/>; and <http://www.kimptonhotels.com/careers/div_topreasons.aspx>.

4. Bill Kimpton quote ("A hotel should relieve travellers…") from "Bill Kimpton—Pioneer Hotel Developer," *Blockbrief News* <http://blog.blockbrief.com/bill-kimpton-pioneer-hotel-developer/>, accessed in April 2013.

5. Kelly Meerbot's story about great service at the Kimpton Hotel in Chicago from an interview with Bernadette Jiwa in January 2013.

6. Information about Kimpton as one of *Fortune* magazine's 100 Best Companies, from "100 Best Companies to Work For: Kimpton Hotels & Restaurants," <http://money.cnn.com/magazines/fortune/best-companies/2013/snapshots/28.html>, accessed in April 2013.

7. Information about MailChimp's more sombre mode from the company website, <http://kb.mailchimp.com/article/how-do-i-make-the-talking-chimp-disappear>.

8. Information about MailChimp customer support from "Scaling Support for 2 Million Users," posted by Bill Bounds, 15 November 2012, on the company blog. <http://blog.mailchimp.com/scaling-support-for-2-million-users/>

9. Chikodi Chima quote from "Creative Cultures: MailChimp Grants Employees 'Permission To Be Creative,'" by Chikodi

Chima, *Fast Company*, 27 July 2011. <http://www.fastcompany.com/1767793/creative-cultures-mailchimp-grants-employees-permission-be-creative>

10. Joseph Flaherty quote from "How Industrial Design and Weird Swag Helped MailChimp Find Success," by Joseph Flaherty, *Wired*, 12 December 2012. <http://www.wired.com/design/2012/12/mailchimp-swag/>

11. MailChimp customer acquisition rate from the company website, <http://mailchimp.com/about/>.

CHAPTER 7: VALUE YOU DELIVER

1. Roger Dooley quotation from *Brainfluence: 100 Ways to Persuade and Convince Consumers with Neuromarketing*, by Roger Dooley. (John Wiley & Sons, 2011.)

2. Information about Snakes & Lattes café from the company website, <http://www.snakesandlattes.com/pages/games>, and from "Introducing: Snakes and Lattes, the Annex's clever new board games café," by Karon Liu, *Toronto Life*, 1 September 2010, <http://www.torontolife.com/daily-dish/

openings/2010/09/01/introducing-snakes-and-lattes-the-
annex%E2%80%99s-clever-new-board-games-cafe/>.

3. Information about Bahen & Co. from Josh Bahen's interview
with Bernadette Jiwa in April 2013.

CHAPTER 8: NAME AND TAGLINE—YOUR OPENING MOVE

1. Branding definition from Lexicon Branding, Inc., website
<http://www.lexiconbranding.com/naming-services/brand-
naming>.

2. Information about the name change from Shoe Site to Zappos from "How I Did It: Tony Hsieh, CEO, Zappos.com", *Inc.*,
1 September 2006. <http://www.inc.com/magazine/20060901/
hidi-hsieh.html>

3. Information about NZ Tax Refunds from the company website, <http://www.nztaxrefunds.co.nz/> and <http://www.nz-
taxrefunds.co.nz/about-us>, and from Cilla Hegarty's interview
with Bernadette Jiwa, 8 April 2013.

4. Information about Nike from "The Forbes Fab 40: The
World's Most Valuable Sports Brands," by Mike Ozanian,
Forbes, 17 October 2012, <http://www.forbes.com/sites/mikeo-

zanian/2012/10/17/the-forbes-fab-40-the-worlds-most-valuable-sports-brands-4/>, and from "Mini-case Study: Nike's 'Just Do It' Advertising Campaign," Centre for Applied Research, <http://www.cfar.com/Documents/nikecmp.pdf>.

CHAPTER 9: CONTENT AND COPY

1. Jason Fried quote from "Why Is Business Writing So Awful?" by Jason Fried, *Inc.*, 1 May 2010. <http://www.inc.com/maga-zine/20100501/why-is-business-writing-so-awful.html>

2. Derek Sivers quotation and text of CD Baby's confirmation email from *Anything You Want: 40 Lessons for a New Kind of Entrepreneur*, by Derek Sivers. (The Domino Project, 2011.) Reprinted with permission.

3. Sales figures and other information about the Old Spice advertising campaign from "Old Spice's agency flexes its bulging stats," by Brian Morrissey, *Adweek*, 4 August 2010. <http://www.adweek.com/adfreak/old-spices-agency-flexes-its-bulging-stats-12396>

CHAPTER 10: DESIGN

1. Christian Louboutin quotation from <http://www.coplons. com/louboutin.html>, accessed in April 2013.

2. Information about Christian Louboutin and the lawsuit from "Red Sole Man: Christian Louboutin's Signature Shoe Has Made Him an Icon," by Sharyn Alfonsi and Nikki Battiste, *ABC News*, 18 November 2011 <http://abcnews.go.com/Business/red-sole-man-christian-louboutins-signature-shoe-made/story?id=14983446#.UWOtuRltJXc>, and from "Christian Louboutin vs. YSL 'Red Soles' Court Case Takes A New Twist," *Huffington Post*, 5 September 2012 <http://www.huffingtonpost.com/2012/09/05/christian-louboutin-ysl-red-soles_n_1857992.html>

3. Information about Justin Gignac and "garbage as art" from Justin's interview with Bernadette Jiwa, 27 November 2012.

CHAPTER 11: YOUR ACTIONS

1. Information about the "100% model" of charity: water from the organization's website, <http://www.charitywater.org/100percent/>.

2. Email messages from veterinarians: private correspondence, shared with the author and used with permission.

CHAPTER 12: CUSTOMER EXPERIENCE

1. Brian Solis quote from "TED Talk: Reinventing Consumer Capitalism—Screw Business as Usual" by Brian Solis, 29 October 2012. <http://www.briansolis.com/2012/10/tedtalk-reinventing-consumer-capitalism-screw-business-as-usual/>

2. Restaurant story and quotes from "Restaurant row goes online after owner gives customer a serve," by Jillian McHugh, *WA Today*, 6 February 2013. <http://www.watoday.com.au/entertainment/your-perth/restaurant-row-goes-online-after-owner-gives-customer-a-serve-20130205-2dwqe.html>

3. Nespresso quote from the Nespresso website, <http://www.nespresso.com/us/en/pages/club-boutique-concept>.

4. Stephanie H's Yelp.com review of a Nespresso store from Stephanie Holt; used with permission.

CHAPTER 13: PRICE AND QUALITY

1. "Stories" quote from Joshua Glenn and Rob Walker, Significant Objects website, <http://significantobjects.com/about/>.

2. Richelle Parham quote from "Objects of Our Desire: The Role of Story in Digital Commerce," video from the Future of

StoryTelling conference 2012. <http://futureofstorytelling.org/film/?id=10>

3. Price of Princess Beatrice's hat when sold at auction, from "Princess Beatrice's royal wedding hat tops $131,341," *Auction Central News*, 23 May 2011. <http://www.auctioncentralnews.com/index.php/features/general-interest/4635-princess-beatrices-royal-wedding-hat-tops-131341>

4. Neil Blumenthal quotations, industry finance figures, and information about hitting the first year's sales targets and selling out the top 15 styles, from "Brand Building Through Narrative and Vulnerability," talk by Neil Blumenthal at PSFK 2013. <http://www.psfk.com/2013/05/neil-blumenthal-warby-parker.html>

5. Warby Parker's mission statement from the "Our Story" page on the company website, <http://www.warbyparker.com/our-story/>.

6. The "well-placed editorials" quote, 500% growth figure, and waiting-list number from "How Warby Parker Grew So Fast: 3 Reasons," by Eric Markowitz. *Inc.*, 7 March 2012. <http://www.inc.com/eric-markowitz/3-reasons-warby-parker-is-killing-it.html>

7. Number of pairs of glasses donated in 2012 from the 2012 Warby Parker Annual Report <http://www.warbyparker.com/annual-report-2012>.

8. Information about the long queue and long wait after the Warby Parker store opened from the "We All Scream For Glasses" post on the company blog, <http://blog.warbyparker.com/post/48119886827/we-all-scream-for-glasses>.

9. Information about glasses as fashion accessories from "Warby Parker Disrupts the Eyewear Industry," a video on Inc.com. <http://www.inc.com/video/2011/success-stories-warby-parker.html>

10. Chobani's revenue figures (shooting from zero to a billion in five years) from Hamdi Ulukaya's talk at the PSFK 2013 NYC conference. <http://www.psfk.com/video/single?video=65761672>

11. Hamdi Ulukaya "when it's authentic" quote from a video on the Chobani website, <http://www.chobani.com/goreal/>.

12. Chobani employment figures from the company website, <http://www.chobani.com/who-we-are/>.

CHAPTER 14: ~~POSITION~~ PERCEPTION

1. Cyber Monday information from "U.S. Online Holiday Shopping Season Reaches Record $32.6 Billion…," *com-Score*, 5 January 2011. <http://www.comscore.com/Insights/Press_Releases/2011/1/U.S._Online_Holiday_Shopping_Season_Reaches_Record_32.6_Billion_for_November_December_Period>

2. Information about Patagonia's "Don't buy this jacket" campaign from "Don't Buy This Jacket, Black Friday, and the New York Times," Patagonia blog, November 2011, <http://www.thecleanestline.com/2011/11/dont-buy-this-jacket-black-friday-and-the-new-york-times.html>.

3. Definition of positioning from *Positioning: The Battle for Your Mind*, by Al Ries and Jack Trout. (McGraw-Hill, 1981.)

4. Information about how the Vespa began from "How Vespas Work," by Ed Grabianowski, for *How Stuff Works*, <http://www.howstuffworks.com/vespa2.htm/printable>, and from "History of the Vespa Scooter," by Monica Marchi, for *EuroGraduateLive*, <http://www.eurograduate.com/lifestyle/article.asp?id=22&pid=5>.

5. Vespa World Day information from <http://www.vespaworlddays2013.com/history>.

6. Sean Greaney quote from "Veni, vidi, vici—Vespa brand profile," by Sean Greaney, *Marketing* magazine, October 2010; posted online 25 December 2011. <http://www.marketingmag.com.au/blogs/veni-vidi-vici-vespa-brand-profile-9134/#.UWnX-FlcqEes>

7. Tiffany sales figures and Michael Kowalski quote from "To Refurbish Its Image, Tiffany Risks Profits," by Ellen Byron, *Wall Street Journal*, 10 January 2007. <http://online.wsj.com/article/SB116836324469271556.html>

CHAPTER 15: DISTRIBUTION

1. Information about factors influencing the demise of Borders from "The End of Borders and the Future of Books," by Ben Austen. *Bloomberg Businessweek*, 10 November 2011. <http://www.businessweek.com/magazine/the-end-of-borders-and-the-future-of-books-11102011.html>

2. Kindle as the foundation of an ecosystem from "How Amazon Makes Money From The Kindle," by Pascal-Emmanuel Gobry. *Business Insider*, 18 October 2011. <http://www.businessinsider.com/kindle-economics-2011-10>

3. Ebook distribution figure from "Amazon shares climb on Kindle e-book optimism," by Alistair Barr. Reuters, 13 February 2013. <http://www.reuters.com/article/2013/02/13/us-amazon-ebooks-idUSBRE91C1IM20130213>

4. Amanda Palmer quotations from "Amanda Palmer: The art of asking," TED talk, February 2013. <http://www.ted.com/talks/amanda_palmer_the_art_of_asking.html>

5. Amanda Palmer released from her recording contract, from "Free at last, free at last," on Amanda Palmer's blog, <http://blog.amandapalmer.net/post/501070649/free-at-last-free-at-last-dear-roadrunner-records>.

6. Nespresso's service-oriented IT architecture information from "MuleSoft and Optaros Help Nespresso Meet Massive Growth Needs with Next-Generation SOA Solution," MuleSoft Case Study. <http://www.mulesoft.com/case-study-nespresso>

7. Nespresso Club information from "Nespresso is still a beautiful business model," Business Models Inc. <http://businessmodelsinc.wordpress.com/2009/10/29/nespresso-is-still-a-beautiful-model/>

8. Information about Nespresso's direct relationship with customers allowing exclusivity and premium pricing, from *Market-*

ing Channels: A Management View, 8th ed. by Bert Rosenbloom. (Cengage Learning, November 2011.)

9. Information about Iconic's three-hour delivery service from the company website, <http://www.theiconic.com.au/>.

CHAPTER 16: LOCATION

1. Information about Burberry's strategic decisions from "Retail-led Strategy by Burberry to Target High Net Worth Individuals in Asia Pacific," by Ashirvad Tomar, *MarketLine*, 27 February 2013. <http://www.marketline.com/blog/retail-led-strategy-by-burberry-to-target-high-net-worth-individuals-in-asia-pacific/>

2. Information on the closing of HMV stores from "HMV To Close UK Stores," by Paul Cashmere. *Noise11*, 15 January 2013. <http://www.noise11.com/news/hmv-to-close-uk-stores-20130115>

3. Number of Facebook users from "Facebook by the numbers: 1.06 billion monthly active users," by Donna Tam. *c|net*, 30 January 2013. <http://news.cnet.com/8301-1023_3-57566550-93/facebook-by-the-numbers-1.06-billion-monthly-active-users/>

4. The phrase "TV-industrial complex" from the "Non-linear media" post on Seth Godin's blog, <http://sethgodin.typepad.com/seths_blog/2006/01/nonlinear_media.html>.

5. Information on Rooftop Honey in Melbourne from the company website, <http://rooftophoney.com.au/index.html>.

6. Information about Rochelle Adonis Cakes and Confections from the company website, <http://rochelleadonis.com/about-us/>.

7. Information about IKEA's retail location strategy from *Strategic Retail Management: Text and International Cases, 2nd ed.* by Joachim Zentes, Dirk Morschett, and Hanna Schramm-Klein. (Gabler Verlag, 2011.)

CHAPTER 17: UBIQUITY OR SCARCITY

1. Instagram as the largest mobile social network in 2011 from "Instagram Becomes The Largest Mobile Social Network," by Jason Keath. *Social Fresh*, 15 December 2011. <http://socialfresh.com/instagram-largest-mobile-social-network/>

2. History of Smallman Guitars from "Australian classical guitars on the world stage," by Michael Stahl, *Qantas Travel Insider*, 28 February 2013. <http://travelinsider.qantas.com.au/australian_classical_guitars_on_the_world_stage.htm>

3. Information on the growth of Starbucks from the company website, <http://news.starbucks.com/article_display.cfm?article_id=454>.

4. Source for number of store closings from "Starbucks Closing 300 Stores, Laying Off Nearly 7,000," by Frank Ahrens, *The Washington Post*, 28 January 2009. <http://voices.washington-post.com/economy-watch/2009/01/starbucks_closing_hundreds_of.html>

5. NYC Starbucks closings during Hurricane Sandy from "Proof that Starbucks is the new public utility: Panic erupts when it closes, even during a hurricane," by Euny Hong, *Quartz*, 29 October 2012. <http://qz.com/21085/why-panic-erupts-over-hurricane-sandy-starbucks-closings-because-its-the-new-public-utility/>

CHAPTER 18: COMMUNITY

1. Smoke signals as the oldest form of visual communication from <http://en.wikipedia.org/wiki/Smoke_signal>.

2. Information on the TV-industrial complex and mass media from the "Non-linear media" post on Seth Godin's blog, <http://sethgodin.typepad.com/seths_blog/2006/01/nonlinear_media.html>.

3. "Where's the dragon" story and Jørgen Vig Knudstorp quotation from <http://zeitgeistglobal.appspot.com/videos/putting-the-pieces-together>.

4. Airbnb statistics from the company website, <https://www.airbnb.com.au/about>.

5. Information about Wish Lists and Airbnb's evolution from search portal to social platform from "How Airbnb Evolved To Focus On Social Rather Than Searches," by Cliff Kuang, *Co.Design*, 2 October 2012. <http://www.fastcodesign.com/1670890/how-airbnb-evolved-to-focus-on-social-rather-than-searches#1>

6. History of "Movember" from the organization's website, <http://au.movember.com/about/history/>, and from "Adam Garone: Healthier men, one moustache at a time," TED talk by Adam Garone, TEDxToronto 2011; video posted November 2012, <http://www.ted.com/talks/adam_garone_healthier_men_one_moustache_at_a_time.html>.

7. Lego's tribe of "Ambassadors" from the company website, <http://aboutus.lego.com/en/lego-group/programs-and-visits/lego-ambassador/>.

8. Information about Starbucks' "My Starbucks Idea" program from <http://mystarbucksidea.force.com/>.

CHAPTER 19: REPUTATION

1. Jeff Bezos quote from "Jeff Bezos on Word-of-Mouth Power," *Bloomberg Businessweek*, 1 August 2004. <http://www.business-week.com/stories/2004-08-01/online-extra-jeff-bezos-on-word-of-mouth-power>

2. Nathan Labenz quote from "The TripAdvisor effect: Are on-line reviews making brands irrelevant?" by Nathan Labenz, 17 September 2011. <http://gigaom.com/2011/09/17/the-tripadvisor-effect-are-online-reviews-making-brands-irrelevant/>

3. Chadwick Martin Bailey survey information from "Don't Underestimate the Impact of Online Guest Reviews," by Judy Melanson, *Inc.*, May 2010. <http://www.greenbook.org/marketing-research.cfm/impact-of-online-guest-reviews>

4. Rachel Botsman quote from "Rachel Botsman: The currency of the new economy is trust," TEDGlobal 2012 talk, posted September 2012. <http://www.ted.com/talks/ rachel_botsman_the_currency_of_the_new_economy_is_trust.html>

5. History of the Tata Nano car from "Game changer," by Marcus Gee. *The Globe and Mail*, 11 April 2008. <http://www.theglobeandmail.com/report-on-business/game-changer/article679039/>

6. Tata Nano car positioning misstep from "Nano: The blemish on Ratan Tata's otherwise brilliant run," by N. Madhavan, *India Today*, 29 January 2013. <http://businesstoday.intoday.in/story/tata-nano-a-blemish-on-ratan-tata-brilliant-record/1/191897.html>

7. Additional information about the Nano car from: "Tata's Nano, the World's Cheapest Car, Is Sputtering," by Siddharth Philip. *Bloomberg Businessweek*, 11 April 2013, <http://www.businessweek.com/articles/2013-04-11/tatas-nano-the-worlds-cheapest-car-is-sputtering>; and from "Learning from Tata's Nano Mistakes," by Matt Eyring. *HBR Blog Network*, 11 January 2011. <http://blogs.hbr.org/cs/2011/01/learning_from_tatas_nano_mista.html>

8. Nano car design awards information from "Tata Nano shines! Wins global design award," Rediff.com, 23 December 2010. <http://www.rediff.com/business/slide-show/slide-show-1-auto-tata-nano-shines-wins-global-design-award/20101223.htm>

9. Information and quotes about the Method brand from the company website, <http://methodhome.com/methodology/our-story/we-are/> and <http://methodhome.com/peopleagainstdirty/>.

10. Eric Ryan quote and Method "cheerleader" information from *Brand Advocates: Turning Enthusiastic Customers Into A Powerful Marketing Force*, by Rob Fuggetta. (Wiley, 2012.)

11. Nathan Aaron's blog: <http://www.methodlust.com/>.

12. Method market share information from "A Soap Maker Sought Compatibility in a Merger Partner," by Rod Kurtz, *The New York Times*, 16 January 2013. <http://www.nytimes. com/2013/01/17/business/smallbusiness/a-founder-of-the-soap- maker-method-discusses-its-sale.html?pagewanted=all&_r=0>

CHAPTER 20: REACTION AND REACH

1. "Pinched from Virgin Atlantic" story from "Virgin Atlantic salt & pepper set is a steal," Richard Branson's blog, 11 November 2011, <http://www.virgin.com/richard-branson/virgin-atlan- tic-salt-pepper-set-is-a-steal>.

2. The fastest-selling paperback of all time, from "'Mummy porn' *Fifty Shades Of Grey* outstrips Harry Potter to become fastest selling paperback of all time," by Paul Bentley. *Daily Mail*, 17 June 2012. <http://www.dailymail.co.uk/news/ article-2160862/Fifty-Shades-Of-Grey-book-outstrips-Harry- Potter-fastest-selling-paperback-time.html>

3. Definition of "market reach" from <http://www.businessdic- tionary.com/definition/market-reach.html>.

4. Information about Orange Boot Bakery from Mark Dyck's interview with Bernadette Jiwa in April 2013.

5. Information about Jamie Oliver from <http://www.jamieoliver.com/about/jamie-oliver-biog> and <http://issuu.com/bellfrog/docs/jamie-oliver-frv-brand-guidelines>.

6. Information about thefts from Jamie Oliver's restaurants from "My customers steal 30,000 napkins a month and even take the toilet fittings, says Jamie Oliver," by Alasdair Glennie. *Daily Mail*, 15 October 2012. <http://www.dailymail.co.uk/tvshowbiz/article-2218293/Jamie-Oliver-My-customers-steal-30-000-napkins-month-toilet-fittings.html>

7. Information about Starbucks loyalty card use from "Starbucks loyalty cards load up profits," by Melissa Allison. *Seattle Times*, 24 January 2013. <http://seattletimes.com/html/businesstechnology/ 2020205455_starbucksearningsxml.html>

CHAPTER 21: THE KEY THAT NOBODY CAN GIVE YOU

1. Samples of serendipitous inventions from "10 Accidental Inventions You Won't Believe," by Marianne English for *How Stuff Works*, <http://www.howstuffworks.com/innovation/inventions/10-accidental-inventions.htm> and from "9 Things

Invented or Discovered by Accident," by the Editors of Publications International, Ltd. for *How Stuff Works,* <http://science.howstuffworks.com/innovation/scientific-experiments/9-things-invented-or-discovered-by-accident.htm>.

2. Definition of "serendipity" from *The Culture Show,* Episode 17, BBC 2, 20 November 2012. <http://www.youtube.com/watch?v=KrNNYSzg88s>

3. Beginnings of Virgin Atlantic from the "Birth of Virgin Atlantic" post on *RaviTheSun,* the blog of Ravi J. Mevcha, <http://ravithesun.wordpress.com/2006/12/25/birth-of-virgin-atlantic/>.

4. Information about the adoptive parents of Steve Jobs and why he didn't finish college from "Steve Jobs Stanford Commencement Speech 2005," <http://www.youtube.com/watch?v=D1R-jKKp3NA>.

5. Information about Yahoo not buying Google when it had the chance from "10 Unusual Things I Didn't Know About Google," by James Altucher, *The Altucher Confidential.* <http://www.jamesaltucher.com/2011/03/10-unusual-things-about-google/>

6. Information about Howard Schultz's visit to Milan from "Howard Schultz and the coffee experience," *Venture Naviga-*

tor, August 2007. <http://www.venturenavigator.co.uk/content/159>

7. Information about Michael Buerk's TV report from Ethiopia in 1984 from "1984: Extent of Ethiopia famine revealed," *BBC News*, 22 October 2009. <http://news.bbc.co.uk/2/hi/in_depth/8315248.stm>

8. R. Gopalakrishnan quote from "The McDonaldisation trap: how managers can benefit from intuition," August 2009. <http://www.tata.com/media/Speeches/inside.aspx?artid=Q2VFdIVGH7o=>

9. P&G advertising figure from *Grow: How Ideals Power Growth and Profit at the World's Greatest Companies*, by Jim Stengel. (Crown Business, 2011.)

10. Information about Dove's "Campaign for Real Beauty" from the company website, <http://www.unileverusa.com/brands-in-action/detail/Dove-/298217/>.

Acknowledgments

The first thing I do when I open a new book, before I even look at the contents, is to read the dedication and the acknowledgements. I know that it takes more than an author to write a book. Somehow, reading the backstory of how the book came to be and who made it possible connects me to the ideas in the book and to the intention of the author.

Many of the ideas in this book were inspired by the genius of Seth Godin. In his blog and his books, Seth was talking about the importance of stories, purple cows, and free prizes a decade ago. We should have been listening back then! He teaches me something every single day. Seth gave me the courage to stand up and say, "here, I made this." I couldn't have started without him.

Thanks to Reese Spykerman for her design genius, for years of partnership and patience, and for helping me to tell the story before a word is read. Thanks to my editor Catherine Oliver for taking the cookie and working with me to tell a better story about the fortune. To Robert Watkins for the nudge on the title. Thanks to the team at TEDxPerth for giving me the opportunity to spread the idea. To David Wang for keeping TheStoryofTelling.com on the road.

To every single person who reads and shares my blog, without you there would be no reason to write. Your dreams and your stories have been the impetus for many 4:30 am starts. You are much more than a blip on Google Analytics to me. To my clients, thank you for allowing me to be part of your journey. It's a joy to watch you telling and living your stories.

To every one of the entrepreneurs and companies featured in this book, thank you for giving me a story to tell. Thanks to the people who gave generously of their time from crazy schedules to read and blurb this book and to Kelly Meerbott and Anna Spargo-Ryan for permission to use their stories.

Thanks to Australia for blue skies and for giving me a place to walk on white sand and find my voice. To my friends Emma Isaacs, Penney Griffiths, Pauline Ryan, Alexx Stuart, Rosie Gray, James Lush and Sue Pickard for their big hearts. Thanks to my Mam and Dad in Dublin for being proud of even the smallest things.

To Moyez, Adam, Kieran, and Matthew, thanks for your love no matter what.

90186970R00120

Made in the USA
Middletown, DE
20 September 2018